The Soul's Way

The Journey of Reincarnation

How Past Lives Affect Your Present Life and Create Your Future Lifetimes

By Ariaa Jaeger

ariaa

A higher way of thinking,
A more evolved way of living
and a more loving way of being.

The Soul's Way: The Journey of Reincarnation
By Ariaa Jaeger

The intent of the author is to offer information of a spiritual and practical nature to help you in your quest for a more fulfilling life. The author does not dispense medical advice, and any practices implemented from reading this book are at the sole discretion of the reader and are not the responsibility of the author.

Crescendo Publishing
Hamilton, ON Canada
1-877-575-8824

ISBN #978-0-9895503-1-4 (sc)
ISBN #978-0-9895503-2-1 (e)

https://www.Ariaa.com

Cover Photography by Christy Leigh Photography
Cover Design by Rupa Limbu

Printed in the United States of America
10 9 8 7 6 5 4 3 2 1

Contents

Dedicated to

To all those beautiful human beings who came
before and have returned time and time again
to make a difference in the world with selfless,
thoughtful acts of kindness and love.

Introduction

"And only the enlightened can recall their former lives; for the rest of us, the memories of past existences are but glints of light, twinges of longing, passing shadows, disturbingly familiar, that are gone before they can be grasped, like the passage of that silver bird on Dhaulagiri."

Peter Matthiessen,
The Snow Leopard

"There is no death. How can there be death if every-thing is part of the Godhead? The soul never dies and the body is never really alive."

Isaac Bashevis Singer,
"Stories from Behind the Stove"

"As far back as I can remember I have unconsciously referred to the experiences of a previous state of existence."

Henry David Thoreau

"I know I am deathless. We have thus far exhausted trillions of winters and summers. There are trillions ahead, and trillions ahead of them."

Walt Whitman

"I am certain that I have been here as I am now a thousand times before, and I hope to return a thousand times."

Goethe

"All human beings go through a previous life... Who knows how many fleshly forms the heir of heaven occupies before he can be brought to understand the value of that silence and solitude whose starry plains are but the vestibule of spiritual worlds?"

Honore de Balzac

"Some people believe that we go on living in another body after death, that we lived before. They call it reincarnation. That we all lived before on the earth thousands of years ago or on some other planet. They say we have forgotten it. Some say they remember their past lives."

Carl Jung

"I hold that when a person dies, his soul returns again to earth; arrayed in some new flesh disguise. Another mother gives him birth with sturdier limbs and a brighter brain."

George Harrison

"It is not more surprising to be born twice than once; everything in nature is resurrection."

Voltaire

Countless scholars and enlightened minds have espoused the theory of reincarnation and, in many cases, demonstrated its relevance in today's world. Innumerable academic studies have effectively proven that reincarnation is real, but some feel science falls short in offering physical proof of the soul's return to Earth. The argument can be made that perhaps, it is somehow intentionally left to the belief or understanding of each individual.

The purpose of this book and my intention is to simply offer a perspective to those seeking answers for their own dilemmas, for which there are no obvious answers. If you are one of those people who've had phantom pain or feelings of loss and guilt without a known cause, shame for no reason, loneliness, depression, unexplained reoccurring dreams, unresolved fears or freakish ailments, addiction, nightmares, or any other unexplained anomalies, this book will find you. If you've felt an instant connection to a stranger, as in a soulmate or twin soul scenario, this book will find you.

The views and opinions in this book are strictly based on my own personal experience as a spiritual life strategist, counselor, regression hypnotherapist, and energy, wellness, and meditation facilitator. The principles and modalities I practice, the wisdom I share, come naturally and flow abundantly following a twenty-seven-minute clinical death in the Alps, in 1993, chronicled in my earlier book, *Ariaaisms*

Spiritual Food for the Soul. Before that profound occasion, I was a vastly different soul with vastly different beliefs and lacked a greater understanding in the areas of mysticism, regression, spiritual science, quantum physics, or spiritual psychology.

My own personal experience with reincarnation didn't come until the day I died and was shown why I'd be returning to Earth to teach, love, inspire, enlighten, and educate those placed in my path and those who choose to expand their consciousness. Like many in my position, I could not imagine why I had been tasked with such an enormous platform. Those who dwell in spirit showed me in ways, hard to define but clear to behold, who I'd been in several pinnacle incarnations. I was shown with clarity how I'd served and what I'd accomplished eons before. Even the humblest person is humbled greater by all that is seen, felt, heard, and absorbed while in that environment. You find your thoughts flow fluidly like a great philosopher.

Repeatedly, the sages—also known as the Masters—would mysteriously beckon: "Remember who you are." Aware that ego has no place in those with an evolved consciousness, I was confused and recognized they were not talking about any particular personality or lifetime but were imploring me to remember all I was absorbing. God is everything and everything is God. That source of quantum love is in every person, every blade of grass, every animal, every tree, and in the atmosphere itself.

While in that paradisiacal paradigm, you know truth when you hear it; in fact, there is no doubt whatsoever. You are in a space of pure love and a frequency which enables comprehensive understanding. Through holographs, which are the records of life's eternal continuum, I viewed my previous roles and knew things I should not know; the remembrance of names, towns, and roles I've played in history came instantaneously. Even unique aromas, like the smell of wet wool mixed with the pungent odor of cow and sheep dung, typically found on Scottish highlanders, was instantly familiar.

Now, viewing my soul's records, things I'd dreamt, felt, and known, suddenly found explanation. Not all of my lifetimes were revealed; some were left for me to uncover later, when my soul was ready and prepared to handle them. Timing is paramount to the unveiling of past life memories. If you are unprepared spiritually, some memories can devastate or cause one to suddenly get stuck in the past.

Wholeness comes from self-discovery and uncovering the totality of who you are. The "why" of your every aspect is invigorating and empowering and worth exploring. You arrived on Earth to heal whatever is left over from other incarnations, to undo the negatives you've put into the world previously, to repay the delayed consequences of actions taken outside the fold of love, and to strip away the strife of yesterday.

Evolving is your job as a human, though it is intrinsically voluntary. No one comes to the Earth without purpose. This is the only place where tangibility is in concert with consciousness. Earth is the great university for all souls longing to navigate the human and spiritual terrain which leads to the highest plateau. When you've found *you* in history books, famous paintings, on the walls of Egyptian pyramids, or in the catacombs of ancient cities, you will feel more confident, more complete, and more accomplished than before. Like pieces of a grand puzzle, when you study the shape and formations of your consciousness and how it evolved through every lifetime, every aspect of you makes perfect sense.

Becoming emotionally, physically, and spiritually the highest version of you frees the flow of life and makes the ride on Earth more joyful. Without learning at least some of who you've been before, you may never become all you're intended to be today.

Prologue

Raised in a small, one-horse town by grandparents who lived and breathed the rhetoric that Southern Baptists served up week after week, I was the least likely candidate to end up teaching this work. While I attended church regularly and often excelled, even memorizing the books of the Bible by age six, accepting Jesus as my Savior and being baptized at the same age, my beliefs did not include anything remotely universal. I'd read some of the world's greatest minds who clearly understood and had insight into the world beyond, but in a small town, you are made to look like a buffoon if you even hint at such "nonsense." Intellect was not highly sought after or valued in this little Texas town.

Dissatisfied with the limited beliefs of the Southern Baptist Church, I began my own spiritual search nine years before this profound death experience occurred. In 1984, I learned to meditate and had embraced a more expanded understanding of Christianity, briefly studying for a degree in Divinity. I was so convinced that meditation was life-transforming that when I started a new job, it was written in my contract that I would get an hour and a half for lunch so I could participate in Unity Church of Christianity's thirty-minute guided meditation every day. I credit those meditations to my personal sojourn, opening doors to spiritual evolution and windows into past lives.

Reincarnation makes sense of life's great mysteries.

The majority of humans will never seek to understand their previous incarnations and continue to blame fate or others for their lot in life, particularly if their life is chock-full of karma. What should be more disturbing than not taking personal responsibility is not being proactive in exploring, searching, offsetting, and addressing negative karma. When major things go wrong, your first question should be, "Why is this happening and what did I do to attract it?"

If you truly search your soul and there is no explanation whatsoever, then it is time to search beyond the present day. That process only works if you are brutally honest with yourself and are ready to face the unknown. Many say they want to know who they've been, but deep inside they fear what they may find. Fear alone will block any memories from surfacing until you heal your fear of the unknown. Most people are more comfortable in their fear than they are in wellness. The goal of a soul returning to life on Earth is to complete the karma, exhaust the drama, and engage the dharma or life's purpose.

Some people actually have a hint or some benign insight into their past. Through dreams or in meditation or even travel to certain familiar places, glances to the past may have been gleaned. Those dramatic or traumatic lifetimes can take years to surface while the fulfilling ones may surface with little effort. Again, there is always divine timing on what comes up.

It is up to each person to retain, activate, or investigate those memories which attempt to surface, at some point, in most spiritually active people. That is typically not the case for those who don't enable belief or infinite possibilities. Those who are fearful or did dastardly things in other lifetimes or suffered great loss and heartache, even though consciously unaware of it, are rarely inclined to acknowledge the validity of reincarnation. While they are not aware of their past lives, the memories remain in the subtle anatomy rather than in the conscious one. Not every lifetime will hold trauma; in fact, the majority will be mundane, nameless, faceless lifetimes which hold ordinary experiences. Not every lifetime will be someone famous or historical; in fact, those are typically a very small percentage.

Not every lifetime will contain negative karma, though the majority will. Negative karma can be anything from negative thoughts or actions toward another to taking a life, including your own. The greater your intention while wielding any action, the more potent the karmic return. You don't need to remember exactly what you did, and I am sure you probably won't. In many cases, there is a knowing, a vague remembrance of something unsavory.

Utilizing regression techniques, hypnosis, focused, targeted prayer, meditation, mindfulness, a host of other therapeutic modalities, and acting upon anything you may be feeling or sensing with deliberation and intention helps access the past. If you suddenly love everything Irish, research Ireland, or watch Irish films. Listen to Irish music and you will trigger the memories. If you are inexplicably drawn back to Italy, plan a trip and learn to speak the language. If you're drawn to Asian, Indian, or Middle Eastern cuisine, make a reservation and dive into those cultures.

The more you pay attention to the subtle anatomy, the more you seek, the quicker the doors of insight begin to open. It is left up to you; nothing will come unless you welcome it in and are emotionally prepared to deal with what you uncover. Unless you open your heart to a world beyond the present, you will remain only half complete—a teapot without a cup, a well without a bucket.

Since my death experience, I have had the immense pleasure of lecturing, counseling, and mentoring some of the most wonderful people you'd ever hope to meet. They have been rich in both depth and texture, the quality of each soul as vast as the oceans of the Earth. I don't advertise or market my spiritual gifts or services, yet those who are intended to find me always do, and some of their stories are remarkable.

Over the years through various modalities, I've facilitated past life regressions and aided others in surfacing their own shadows from lifetimes gone by. Unlike some in my field, I encourage memories to surface in ways that validate the client's own experiences and intuition, as opposed to psychically giving them the answers. With their permission, this book includes a few of their stories and how they found healing in the most remarkable ways through viewing their own past. Names have been changed to protect their identity, but the facts of each story are accurate.

There are innumerable academic studies and qualified authors in this space who can cite reams of data and cases where reincarnation has been validated and authenticated. The market is flooded with books on scientifically measured cases, but the book you hold in your hands offers a more lilting, loving, and digestible perspective.

This book is not meant to convince you of anything. This is about your own personal journey; you decide how deep to delve into self-realization and past life discovery, and only you determine how much you wish to know and heal. Take what works for you and discard the rest. My hope is that it launches you on your own path to healing and inspires you to explore and investigate the paths you've walked, thus expanding your consciousness while increasing your frequency.

The higher your frequency, the more open you are, the more you will see. Studies have shown that every living thing has a vibration and an effect on neurobiology. The higher your vibration, the more limitless and healthier you become, and the more attuned you are to worlds beyond the present.

Don't get impatient; there is a rhythm to accessing the past and, typically, only the most pertinent lifetime memories will surface. Specificity and consistency lay the groundwork while research and details will complete the puzzle.

Inhabiting Earth is far more enriching when you are emotionally and physically healthy. While the life you're living today is paramount to creating your own wellness, your past lives are a working blueprint, the epicenter of your own well-being. There is a universe living inside every human being. The search for the understanding of oneself is the single most important goal you can accomplish while on Earth.

It is that important. You are that important.

Chapter 1

Walking History

Why does it matter who you have been in other incarnations? What difference does it make? I compare it to leaving the yeast out of a bread recipe. Without some knowledge of lives which have impacted, influenced, or inhibited the life you are living today, your life is basically flat and one-dimensional. There are explanations for your unusual fears, idiosyncrasies, and even phantom pain. There are worlds inside of you waiting to be discovered and explored.

People walk around the Earth feeling victimized by the government, their circumstances, their karma, and their health, never realizing that all of it is an extension of the past. Seldom are physical and emotional injuries a first-time occurrence. Anger and rage without an obvious cause, feelings of abandonment, deep-seated fears of drowning, fire, rape, being murdered, dogs, or other animals, and so on, fall under the category of cellular memory.

A cellular memory is a multiple lifetime imprint from previous physical and emotional trauma. If it goes unhealed, you are susceptible to compounding it in subsequent lifetimes and even today. What goes unhealed slowly surfaces, giving the human being an opportunity to evaluate, elevate, integrate, and evolve. As a society, humans are more in touch with their feelings, emotions, and spirituality than ever before.

Since only 25 percent of the world's population believes in reincarnation, many will never understand why they are dismissed at their doctor's office as being hypochondriac or their symptoms labeled psychosomatic. Many are misdiagnosed with some form of mental illness when what they are experiencing may in fact be a past life memory surfacing. Additionally, how you live in this lifetime will determine the quality of the life you have in your next incarnation. Karma plays a role, as does passion, interests, and soul group clearing, or gathering to support each other again.

The notion of reincarnation is as old as time, but the first references to it only began to surface about 2600 years ago. Theories about reincarnation began in Northern India somewhere between 1000-600 BC. Around 570 BC, the Greek philosopher and mathematician Pythagoras was born. As a young man, he published that the soul was immortal and after the death of the body, the soul could return to another body. In the 5th century, the Greek philosopher, Plato, taught his students that the soul is born many times and can be here for as many as 10,000 years before returning to heaven. (Inaccurate, but I love that he opened the door to understanding reincarnation.)

Over the years, the theory of reincarnation has been widely accepted in eastern cultures but was quietly introduced in the western world in the 19th century. Hinduism was introduced in the United States by the Indian teacher Swami Vivekananda (1863-1902). In 1895, the Swami established the Vedanta Society, whose primary focus was on reincarnation.

A host of others came before and after, including Ukrainian Helena Blavatsky (1831-1891) along with American Henry Steel Olcott (1832-1907), who, together, founded the New York Theosophical Society in 1875. By the early 1900s, there were a host of new religions born worldwide, and many accepted the concept of reincarnation.

There are also many passages in the Bible which allude to and often directly speak of reincarnation.

Upon speaking about Elijah, Jesus said:

"But I tell you, Elijah has come, and they have done to him everything they wished, just as it is written about him." *(Mark 9:13)*

Jesus was referring to this early prophecy:

"See, I will send you the prophet Elijah before that great and dreadful day of the LORD comes." *(Malachi 4:5)*

"For all the prophets and the law prophesied until John. And if you are willing to accept it, ***he is the Elijah*** *who was to come." (Matt 11:13-14)*

*"But I tell you, **Elijah has already come**, and they did not recognize him..." Then the disciples understood that he was talking to them about **John the Baptist**. (Matt 17:12-13)*

*But the angel said to him "do not be afraid, Zechariah; your wife Elizabeth will bear you a son, and you are to give him the name John...And he will go on before the Lord, in the **spirit and power of Elijah**...to make ready a people prepared for the Lord." (Luke 1:13 & 17)*

I have always considered it simple common sense, given that it would be virtually impossible to arrive on Earth and be expected to get it right the first and only time. With a Southern Baptist upbringing replete with fire and damnation, it wasn't until my death in the Alps that my suspicions about reincarnation were truly validated.

The teachings of Jesus emphasize the necessitation of forgiveness, but if you live a perfect life from start to finish in only one lifetime, the theory is moot. Additionally, the idea that Jesus would die to reconcile human sins when he never experienced any sin at all is absurd. Edgar Cayce, the "sleeping prophet," chronicled some of the other lives of Jesus demonstrating how Jesus learned many of the lessons we as human beings experience every day. The truest wisdom always comes from your own personal experience, which is why I am so emphatic and personally passionate about meditation.

Accessing some of your own lifetimes is far less complicated than most realize. Reconciling memories from another existence with your life today can be incredibly challenging. When you become aware of who you've been previously, you often find the loss and longing of those days gone by haunting. I've been known to drop everything to travel back in time, so to speak, by booking a "return" trip to places I've roamed when memories are predominantly waking.

Walking your own history is exuberating! The comfort or discomfort, in some cases is reveling and you're often flooded with names, dates, and events, in your dreams. Dreams are often the only way Spirit can speak to you if you are not an avid meditator. The questions you ask, the intensity with which you seek the answers to your own lifetimes, is just as important as the answers that follow.

Right after my surreal death experience and subsequent return to the earthly plane, I became aware of my most recent past lifetime, and it was in the very region where this profound metamorphosis took place. I longed and pined to return to the home I loved so much and to set my feet back on the grounds where I had walked less than fifty years earlier. The memories flooded my mind and haunted me. My husband was keenly aware of my visions and the specific dreams I had, which showed me my previous home in Austria, complete with steeples and gables. We did some research at a local library (cell phones and Google did not exist at that time), which led to its location, and we made two attempts in two years to visit the hallowed grounds I knew and loved.

Naturally, strange things happened.

On the first trip, I fell into a trance-like deep sleep as my husband navigated the small lakeside roads. After several attempts, he was unable to awaken me, so he turned the car around and drove back to our bed and breakfast more than an hour away. Minutes before we arrived, I suddenly woke up as if I'd never been asleep. My husband was in the infancy stages of learning how to live with a mystic and the stranger than strange things which accompanied it.

The following year, we returned to Austria in May. We didn't waste any time, and after recovering sufficiently from jet lag, we attempted the road trip to my former dwelling once again. As if a note out of sync in the orchestra of life, I fell into a slumber once again as we drove the now familiar road. This time, I was prepared with coffee and Red Bull in hand and was determined to stay awake as we neared "home." We made it to the house or castle, as many deemed it and as we got out of the car, a surly-looking woman shot out of the house and began screaming at us, "You're trespassing!"

I was mortified and tried to explain in a childlike voice that we just wanted to walk down to the lake. She couldn't have known I had spent a lifetime there, and frankly she didn't care as she firmly and rudely shooed us away. I was so dismayed and frustrated to be ordered off my own property, my present-day ego in direct clash with my past life ego. At the risk of sounding cliché, there is a reason for everything and always a divine timing on all memories. Additionally, I had staved off the trancelike sleep which would have prevented this negative encounter, but the universe always finds a way to exact the antidote. Heavy-hearted and disappointed, I succumbed to the flow.

Finally, the following year, after meditating repeatedly about revisiting the past, we felt the time was right. So, for a third time, we mustered the courage to make the drive. I was apprehensive, given how we were received the previous year, but I knew I desperately needed closure on so many events from that era. Anticipation filled every bone in my body as we returned, determined and convicted to enter this ghostly dwelling to see if the walls would talk and speak they did.

We arrived on a beautiful Austrian summer afternoon. The sun was kissing the bluish-green lake with an inviting glow, shimmering like thousands of Swarovski crystals. We walked up to the door and rang the bell, and to our surprise, the owner of this palatial estate opened the door with a warm, friendly smile, almost as if she knew me. The lovely, small framed, Austrian Frau immediately and graciously invited us in, without any hesitation.

I scurried to look around, not just because my soul was craven, but I was afraid the old curmudgeon we'd encountered on our previous visit might be inside. To our credit, we didn't mention that we were ordered off her property the year before.

Like my anticipatory heart, she swung the heavy wooden door wide open, and I leapt across the foyer, as if I were a dancing sprite with wings lighter than air. We mentioned how enamored we were with the architecture and asked if we might be allowed to take a tour, to which she pleasantly complied. She told us that she had been thinking of selling the place, which was now considered a national historical site. The asking price was a mere 3.1 million dollars. What I wouldn't have paid to own the place today, which had brought me so much joy in yesteryear. I pined at why I had not been born rich so I could reclaim what was rightfully mine...but then remembered, you cannot go backward or tarry with yesterday.

As we walked the halls and glimpsed the rooms, time did tarry backward; it was surreal. I could "see" myself dressed in expensive clothing which I had crafted with my own hands. I was a well-known fashion designer who catered to the upper crust and aristocracy of Austria in the late 1800s and early 1900s, and even designed clothing for the Royal family of Austria.

The great love of my life from that period of time was an acclaimed artist but also a bit of a cad, having more concubines and illegitimate children than common sense. We never married, nor did we ever consummate our relationship. I was the only woman in the world he'd never bedded, or at least it felt that way. History books were kind to us and lavished their praise on both of our works of the time. It is of no surprise that I was considered mystical and leaned toward spiritual teachings then, as I do today. It is historically recorded that I was his "higher love," and the romance was palatable; letters, cards, and hand-holding were daily food, and we both thrived on nuances and romantic innuendo. It was tantamount to perfect love.

Now, as I gazed into the parlor where we once sat having wine and conversation, I could see his ghostly imprint leaning against the mantle of the fireplace, wearing the stylish smock I had fashioned for him. His scent still lingered in every room; the aroma was intoxicating. The memories flooded and overwhelmed me, I could not breathe deep enough; it was as if all the oxygen had left the room and my lungs.

As we walked and talked, the owner showed us pictures of *me* and *him*, leaving me dizzy and slightly faint. She continued with stories of our lives in the mansion, and with every word, tears puddled in my soul. I thought I would drown from inside out.

In a multitude of photos, there I was, from the early 1900s, alive and well, gilded in baroque picture frames. The remembrance of "us," of our perfect love, had been preserved—not only in this house we loved, but in books that graced the Cherrywood bookcases. I was moved to tears but tried to hide them for fear of being discovered. My heart skipped beats and my pulse raced with anticipation as we waltzed in and out of time. How would anyone ever be able to forget such great love? Love always lives on.

It is abundantly clear that our previous lifetimes know not time or space...the memories were as fresh as if they'd occurred yesterday. The universe, in all its divine design, had to have known how difficult it would be if everyone could remember even a tenth of the personalities and lives they have lived. If we could consciously remember the past and how deeply we've loved before, I am convinced none would feel unloved today. I cannot say it too often or too much: love transcends time and always lives on.

I could have lingered for days in this beautiful time warp, my soul insatiable and hungering for one last glimpse in time. But a permanent goodbye was beckoning. With a heart filled to eruption, my soul drowning in loss yet flooded with love, my mind filled to overflow, and my feet weighted by the gravity of yesteryear, we left and drove in silence back into the 20th century.

Chapter 2

Love Lives On

I had been working with a rather challenging client for a few months when she began referring her friends and family to me.

Emma's younger sister, Annie, was about to have yet another surgery on her wedding finger, her fourth in two years. She bore a scar all the way up her wrist from tendon removal surgery and was just thirty-three years old. Not only was she concerned that her finger would never work again, but she had boyfriend issues. She was madly in love but so unhappy and terribly fearful of marriage, yet she could not bring herself to leave her boyfriend of five years.

When we met, I was struck by her beauty—a down-to-earth, tall, slender woman with dark hair and deep-set brown eyes. She was stunning, yet the underlying shadow of her past lives rendered her an insecure, needy, and somewhat awkward host. She cried week after week, every session, her constant insecurities and fears pouring like rain.

At the end of her very first session, as is typical with those integrating previous lifetimes, the door to the past opened. As we sat meditating, I "saw" her dressed in vintage clothing and instinctively knew that she and her daughter had survived the Titanic disaster in 1914. As she sat before me with her eyes closed, an image came into focus. I "saw" her dangling from the ship's enormous anchor chain with her left hand, while trying to hold on to her daughter with her right one. The giant sinking vessel suddenly shifted as it broke in half, the upper bow bobbing like a top, tossing soaked passengers into the icy waters of the Atlantic Ocean. It was while she was holding on with her left hand that the huge anchor ensnarled her finger, crushing it between the hull and the anchor. As she struggled to free her hand, her wedding ring was yanked right off, tumbling to the ocean floor. Once freed, she and her daughter descended into one of the last lifeboats, where they were ferried to safety.

Her husband, standing on the deck with the other men, sadly did not survive. Though not immediate, she was not immune to seeing the symbology of losing both her husband and her wedding ring at the same time. I was certain that Annie's fear of marrying her current boyfriend was rooted in this tragic and sudden loss. She opened her eyes at the end of the mediation, and I began to describe what I'd seen. Tears began flowing, and it was clear I'd triggered something so profoundly deep that she began to wail uncontrollably.

Without a moment's hesitation, we ran to my desk. I didn't look on the first class list of passengers or even the third class, but intuitively knew I would find her on the list of second class passengers. Her previous name intuitively popped into my head the minute I sat down at the computer. As I scoured through the list, I pondered the impact of validating this tragic event and how it might affect her.

Lo and behold, there she was, in a picture taken the day they boarded Titanic, with her eight-year-old daughter in hand and with eerily similar facial and physical features! We found the news story of her and her daughter's survival and a picture of her husband, who was lost that night. The resemblance to her today was striking, and even though there was very little written about her at the time we searched, what was chronicled validated Annie's feelings, fears, and issues of today. We had a name to go with the fear and the trauma. We also discovered that her daughter then was now her older sister, Emma. The resemblance of Emma's previous incarnation to today's appearance was again uncanny.

We spent the next few months working on releasing Annie's fear and healing the wounds and abandonment issues. We addressed the anger of loss and grief, uncovered other lifetimes that compounded her crystallized fears and those which prevented her from wanting to marry today. Annie was, in effect, still grieving the loss of her husband, harboring anger at being left to raise a child in an unforgiving time for women. Her life after Titanic was short, full of trials and pain, and she died very young. Of course she didn't want to marry her current-day boyfriend of five years, Luke. In the subtle anatomy, she still resented him, stoked in fear of losing him again, and the pain of loss was simply too great to risk again.

A year later, we revisited some of her core issues and did another Google search. We were amazed to discover that in that year, an enormous amount of information on her previous life had been uploaded to the internet. Timing and validation appeared once again. A year earlier, she hadn't been prepared to handle the totality of events which took place so long ago. Annie had now processed enough that she was ready to delve deeper in search of the lingering shadows of her past.

Loss is a cruel beast, and most have lost loved ones in historically horrific ways, which have left an indelible mark on the psyche. I am always surprised that people don't realize how much reincarnation plays a role in how they feel and act today, and in their core dysfunction.

Annie returned home that evening to Luke, her boyfriend, who was the very same soul of the husband she'd lost on Titanic, though at that point she only suspected it. She slowly began telling Luke what had happened in her first session and felt that the pieces of the puzzle were beginning to fall into place. She reconciled her behavior of today with her fears of yesteryear and internal healing began. In quiet disbelief, Luke had little to say.

Annie kept her suspicions to herself, still processing her own epiphanies. She started having dreams which validated the information that came in her first session and in subsequent sessions. After using energy work and other modalities week to week, she was finally ready to have the surgery on her finger to repair the compounded injury. The surgery was a success.

Each week, she shared some of what occurred in our sessions with Luke, who dismissed me and the information as nuts. He was vehement that I was a charlatan or a snake oil salesman, something every psychic or those who teach spirituality has had to deal with at some point. But it turns out he was hiding a deep, dark secret, one that would surface in the most unexpected of ways.

For weeks, Annie's fear of loss and matrimony continued to consume our sessions. Luke and Annie had a tumultuous relationship, one which had become toxic. I told Annie that when and if she ever left Luke, she would meet the man of her dreams shortly thereafter. Having spiritually awakened, now practicing meditation regularly and eliminating some of her insecurities and fears, she finally left Luke a few months later. Within a few short weeks, she met the man I mentioned and they embarked on a passionate romance. I wish I could tell you they enjoyed a healthy, happy, and whole relationship, but it was anything but. Brent was a continuation of Luke, lovely on the outside, but the inside was chock-full of issues which added fuel to Annie's internal smoldering fire. He was a reflection of all which remained unhealed in her, a lesson everyone should embrace. Everything is just a reflection of you.

After a year off from session work, she returned for weekly counseling because she was dragging some of her unhealed emotions into this new relationship with Brent. The only difference this time was that she *did* want to get married but was already damaging the relationship, projecting her old wounds onto Brent. He was not the best at handling her emotional outbursts and seemed to be cold and indifferent, eventually becoming very controlling, condescending, and demanding.

She phoned one evening to tell me that Luke was pining and depressed over her new relationship. Even though it had been a year since they split, he simply could not let go and was continuing to text her. She was worried it would interfere with her relationship with Brent but was also concerned for Luke; she even mentioned that he was acting suicidal. She was in disbelief when Luke, distraught and massively depressed, asked for my phone number.

The farmer who thought I was a charlatan only a year earlier was now asking to see me and was willing to drive almost six hours round trip week after week to do so. After a lengthy phone consult, Luke booked an appointment, not knowing what to expect but needing help so desperately, he was willing to go out on a limb.

Luke's first session was revealing and full of insight. This unassuming, third-generation farmer sat listening intently through his tears. By the end of the session, I was sure that he was indeed George Armstrong Faring, the man who had boarded the huge, unsinkable vessel, in hopes of reaching the Americas and a new life that would never be. He continued to sob through the session until it was time to meditate. He claimed he had never meditated before and was awkward, not knowing what to expect.

I began. Typically, I close my eyes as I am leading someone in meditation. But for some reason, this time I peeked.

Suddenly before me, this round-faced, optical lens wearing, rotund farmer became a Buddha-like figure, still and serene. It was as if he had been meditating all his life. I was pleasantly surprised.

After about twenty minutes, he opened his eyes and his face shone like a lightbulb. He looked completely different. The stress and worry had abandoned his face, and his eyes sparkled with a new light. I've seen many a soul transformed in my living room, but this was one of the fastest visual transformations I'd ever witnessed. To my surprise and delight, he began to tell me what he saw in meditation; the colors and images were crystal clear. He left my house that night in such a beautiful state of peace, but only after hugging me for what seemed like an hour.

It was his second session, however, that left me speechless. We uncovered a few more pinnacle lifetimes and gathered greater understanding about the reactions Luke and Annie had to each other. Much of his past life aboard Titanic correlated with his present. It was only in this second session that he felt comfortable enough to tell me the secret he'd been keeping from me.

We returned to the topic of Titanic and he sheepishly began revealing that as a young boy, he was haunted by the story of Titanic, so much so that he had already visited the museum where many of the actual artifacts are on display—not once, but twice. As a second-class passenger on Titanic, George Faring had just sold everything in his small town in England to begin a new life in America. He was actively involved in the church, owned a grocery store, and was loved by the entire town. He was so beloved that after his death, they erected a memorial to him in England, which still stands today.

Some of the Faring's friends had moved to America and began fruit farming. They wrote about the amazing climate and how happy they were in their newfound country. His young wife Camille soon became ill with tuberculosis, so they decided a new beginning and a new climate would help. With their eight-year-old daughter in tow, they embarked on a journey to America aboard the unsinkable Titanic. The parallel of Luke being a third-generation farmer in Colorado was on point, as if he picked up his life today where he left off in that one.

As I led Luke into another meditation, his face began to morph. Suddenly, we were bathed in cascading light so golden in color, it left me speechless. I didn't move—I didn't dare open my eyes—yet the golden color was intense and bled through my closed eyelids. I was in such a state of awe that I almost forgot that Luke was in the room. It was so powerful and so beautiful that I wanted to linger in its enveloping hue and feel the caress of its warmth, to the core of my being. I wondered, who was this man and why such an elaborate display? We were consumed. We opened our eyes and, almost as if in a trance, spoke few words as he walked out the door with a strange energy and look about him. I knew he was overwhelmed and that his three-hour drive back home was going to be longer than usual.

Within 20 minutes he called, and in a slightly frightened voice, he said, "Ariaa, is that normal? I saw this huge golden light and felt this calm peace and incredible feeling. It was more than love." He continued, "I knew if I opened my eyes, it would go away, and I didn't want to lose the feeling!" He was experiencing a phenomenon which only occurs in a handful of people, and most of the time they are spiritually evolved.

Surprisingly, that was not the only grand display in his new spiritual awakening. Week after week, strange, mystical, and magical things unfolded. Whether the universe, his guides, or something greater was trying to convince him of these heavenly paradigms, I cannot say. Whatever was at work was definitely otherworldly.

Luke had decided to return to Las Vegas only six weeks after starting his sessions with me. For the third time, he was going to the exhibition that held such a tight grip on the secrets of his present-day heart. The love he had for Annie was potent, yet self-destructive. This time was going to be different, because now, he was going with the awakened knowledge of his former self.

I gave him a series of suggestions, including asking him to avoid drinking alcohol the night he arrived because it reduces the senses and intuitive abilities. I also suggested he get up bright and early and arrive at the exhibition when they opened.

As with my entire life's work, prayer is a key element to creating, so we prayed intensely for a sign to validate his emotions and journey. He insisted that he didn't need proof, stating that he had somehow known, all his life that he was on that ill-fated vessel. While he felt his reality to the depths of his core, it took time to reconcile his beliefs with his modern-day life. Remember, until he started working with me, he did not believe in reincarnation or anything remotely spiritual. He never read a Bible, never went to church, never learned to meditate, and shunned anything that had to do with the mystical.

The next morning, I waited patiently for his text. Ten minutes later than we planned, he texted to say he was running late but was now on his way. He arrived at the museum to find a couple in front of him and shrugged it off, even though I had emphatically urged him to be the first person in line. Luke entered the exhibition and, as before, he and the couple in front of him were handed the boarding pass of one of Titanic's passengers. The couple began making their way to the first display, which was a list of all the passengers who died when Titanic sank.

Suddenly, the wife turned to her husband but "accidentally" overshot her view and glimpsed Luke's eyes. "There's George Armstrong Faring!"

Startled and chilled to the bone, Luke started to reply, but the shock of someone calling out his past life's name prevented him from speaking. The woman, who was first in line, was actually holding "*his*" boarding pass and had just found Mr. Faring's name on the passenger list. Had Luke arrived when I suggested just minutes earlier, *he* would have been holding his own boarding pass to his previous incarnation. One thousand, five hundred and seventeen souls perished that night. What were the odds that he would be holding his own boarding pass or that someone would call out his previous name aloud?

It fazed him a little, but it didn't seem to matter to Luke. After all, he had been there several times previously, but nothing like this had ever happened before. He was in awe, and it was just the sort of thing you could not dismiss as coincidence— although, no one with any spiritual acumen believes in coincidence anyway.

George Armstrong Faring may have died along with 1,517 others on Titanic that dreadful night, but more than a hundred years later, he is alive and well and living in America today. From death to life, he completed his journey and made it to America to become the farmer he once dreamed of being. He is emotionally healthier than he has ever been and has continued to thrive on American soil.

One of the most famous and well-studied cases of reincarnation is that of Jenny. In 1993, author Jenny Cockell released her book *Yesterday's Children*, chronicling her journey and search for the children she left behind in her last lifetime. As a guest on *Oprah Winfrey*, *Phil Donahue*, and several other talk shows, she revealed that she was formerly Mary Sutton of Malahide, Ireland. Mary died giving birth to her eighth child in the 1930s, twenty-one years before Jenny Cockell was born.

From early childhood on, Jenny had dreams, visions, and memories of her lost children. Through a series of events and hypnosis, the story *Yesterday's Children* emerged, recounting Jenny's return to Ireland to locate her long-lost children. It is a heartwarming tale which leads to an eventual reunion with those children, who at the time were in their sixties and seventies. The most surprising part was that several of the elderly adults fully embraced and accepted this younger woman as their former mother. A few of the others had their own interpretation of Jenny's memories, but in the end, they found resolve and a sense of peace.

The children have all since died, but emotions were the forbearer of this reunion and it is the emotions which lead us back to yesteryear. Memories often carry over into the next lifetime, and in Mary's case, they were pronounced. The book *Yesterday's Children* was made into a powerful movie starring Jane Seymour and aired on network television in 2000.

Today, Jenny continues to write and carry her message about reincarnation into the world. She has explored many other memories of previous lifetimes, making peace with each as she goes. She has expanded her studies to connect the worlds of science and past life memories or consciousness as we know it. We are "friends" on Facebook, and I find her to be one of the most authentic and well-versed people I've ever encountered. Her story inspired a more open awareness and discussion of reincarnation and has led to millions searching to find the answers of their own previous incarnations. She is a pioneer in this field, and her continued work has led to some fascinating discoveries in others.

When it comes to past life memories, emotions, mannerisms, the oddest occurrence, ritual, or habit is often what we retain deep in our consciousness. Most won't remember their full name, only pieces of it like Jenny. She remembered Mary and Malahide, Ireland, but did not remember her surname or the individual names of the children, only their traits and personalities. She remembered places and events and even scents and aromas of the day, but not addresses or birthdates. That is typical in most who recover some of their previous incarnations, which is why a facilitator is so helpful.

It has been my personal experience, and that of clients I have aided over the years, that once you have a sense of something, there are modalities which will help elevate and recover the memories. Dreams are often a great avenue for revelations, as is hypnosis, breathwork, and regression, but actually researching and returning to the place of origin is far more impactful for raising, healing, and integrating memories.

We are not designed to remember the fullness of our previous lives; it would be too difficult, too painful, and many would hunger for what has since passed. We are designed, however, to be able to tap into our deepest consciousness and the emotions which almost always linger today; not to suffer or relive the pain, but to bring light to it and heal those leftover emotions which cast shadows over a present life of well-being or a lack of it.

Love lives on no matter how long or how many lifetimes you transverse the universe. Love is the most concentrated energy in the universe; conversely, so is the energy of hate. However, I find it incredibly reassuring that no one, not even your pets, is ever lost to you. We return time and time again, interacting with many of the same souls in our soul group, and sometimes those outside of it. We amass more light with every return to Earth by mere virtue of re-entering the atmosphere.

It is then incumbent on you to grow your light and energy and to learn how to sustain it. Sustaining light and higher frequency enables the space in-between worlds. The more you seek, the more you'll find and the greater the expanse when you're attuned to a loving heart and an open mind.

The love you give, the love you get, the love you send, and the love you imprint in innumerable ways always remains. This love encircles you like a halo and functions and fluctuates as energy and frequency. It is the consummate constant in an ever-changing universe. Nothing erases or diminishes its potency. It can be said that love is the compass of life; it navigates and leads you to the greatest challenges. It delivers epic trials to forage, prune, harvest, and extract the sweetest nectar from your life's bouquet.

It is the very composition of your soul, the foundation to build upon. Anything less than love's supreme fertilizer takes you farther away from the oneness root. Like a majestic oak tree, with branches that reach for the sky, the succession of the soul is the same. The lower branches of a tree run akin to the lives that came before; they tend to die off unless someone or something does a bit of pruning to activate new growth.

Many will simply work out the details of previous life trauma in a non-conscious or subconscious way, such as dreaming, and most will never even want to know what transpired before. The key to self-awareness lies in those fields and layers of previous incarnations. Often, one doesn't fully know themselves until they explore at least their most impactive lifetimes. They exercise their body to stay fit, but rarely exercise their consciousness to stay emotionally healthy and spiritually evolved. Exploring what came before, especially the most poignant and powerful lives, leads to understanding yourself today and lays the foundation for the next time you decide to return. If you heal it today, it will not travel back with you the next time you return to Earth.

Chapter 3

Coaching Rembrandt

It was a cold, crisp morning, and the dew had hardened into ice crystals kissing the dying blades of grass. Winter was beckoning. My desktop computer was pinging with the sound of a Skype call coming in.

The face of a young man with pinkish skin and a faded shade of red hair came into focus, his eyes like those of a timeless master. He was meager in his ways and yet had a depth that was effortless. His eyes were soft and the color of the sky, yet you could see the lingering imprint of sadness in them. He looked so impish and young, yet inside the shell was an old soul. The banter was lighter than with most of those who seek my help. A young, successful professional with a major name brand corporation, it was apparent he was reluctant to go into any core issues with me just yet. Clearly trust was something I would have to earn.

As his first session unfolded, I wondered what this gentle old soul could be harboring; he seemed very astute for someone seeking spiritual guidance, almost as if it was an afterthought.

The time seemed to sail by, and as with all my clients, I ended with a chakra meditation, a great way for me to transfer and infuse light into core energy centers, which typically sparks an awakening and a deeper level of awareness.

With most clients, I usually open my eyes while they sit in the silent part of the meditation. With the gift of second sight, I "see" what may be attached or what they may be processing. It is also a wonderful way to assess if there are any health-related issues, which may be a contributing factor to whatever issues they are currently dealing with.

Over the decades, I've foreseen events which then manifested weeks, even years later. Seeing through the eyes of time is a gift which academia cannot teach, and is always riveting my own brain, often in direct opposition with the internal aspects of the higher self. My mind is saying, "Holy cow! Amazing!" while my spiritual self is silently in humble bow. I often impulsively grab for my cell phone to snap a picture, and then remember it is impossible to photograph what I am seeing over the face of the person in the room.

I am often asked how I know who I see layered over the face of the person with whom I am working. The answer is quite simple. I don't know until I ask internally, "Who is that?" If I hear the answer, the client is intended to know; otherwise, they may be shown in their dreams or meditations, which is far more powerful than being told.

My emphasis is always on empowering others in how to access their own power and intuition rather than telling them outright. In about 90 percent of all cases, I typically have no knowledge of the personalities they have been. Meaning, they are not people I've studied in school or have read a biographical history on. One of the ways a modern-day mystic or psychic gauges their accuracy is if there is no conscious awareness of what comes through in a reading. Since my own profound heavenly experience, I have been witness to things so dramatic that human minds would be thrown into an instant fit of cynicism, with a dash of denial, served with a heaping side of disbelief.

There is always a perfect timing on knowing who you were in other incarnations, because learning of your own history can often reset the damage done in those lifetimes. A good place to start is to become self-aware and address and heal any current day manifestations. While many anomalies are a compounded extension of past lives, dealing with the immediate emotional issues from this lifetime is a helpful place to begin.

For me, there is no such thing as a "normal" dinner or the simple joys of having "normal friends." I imagine it is the same for anyone with a heightened state of intuition and a coffer full of consciousness. At any dinner party, you are the elephant in the room. It is virtually impossible to "fit in" since the energy around you is often chill-producing. An empath also picks up on the needs and the dysfunction of those in the room and so much more. The unexplainable happens more times than I can share, and often, I am just as baffled as those around me.

Right after the mortgage crisis in America where up to ten million homeowners were either unable to pay their skyrocketing mortgage or were under water, I decided to rent. I had done nothing wrong, had an exceptional credit score, and never missed or was late on a payment. But the banks in America were not as honest and caused millions to lose their homes by no fault of their own. *The Big Short: Inside the Doomsday Machine*, by Michael Lewis, showed how the financial crisis in 2007 was triggered by the United States housing bubble. The film, *The Big Short*, directed by Adam McKay, was released in 2015 to widespread acclaim.

After the painful decision to sell my home, I decided to rent instead and wait until the market stabilized. I found a small home in a great neighborhood and though it was built in 1983 and had some issues, I bought the place after eight years of renting.

Months later, I had a stark dream that caused me to wake up with my heart racing. In the dream, I saw the tops of the trees around me on fire, and I was screaming, "Call 911!" The next day, I called several of my friends and colleagues to discuss this dream because it was simply too real to ignore. The general consensus was to pay attention as it appeared to be a precognitive dream, a dream that happens within 72 hours.

We had extremely high winds the following day, typical for the Colorado Front Range, but they were blowing in a circular motion. During the middle of the night, every alarm in the house began sounding. The smoke detectors, the carbon monoxide detectors, and even the burglar alarm were all clamoring. I leapt from the bed, ran downstairs, and tried to figure out why, to no avail. After an hour, they suddenly stopped. After investigating and finding nothing, I changed the batteries in the smoke detectors and returned to bed.

The next day, to my surprise, they began chirping—small, intermittent beeps which annoyed my four dogs to no end. It went on all day long, then I suddenly remembered my dream! I called 911 and sheepishly told them I was unsure why the alarms were going off because I could not detect fire. Within minutes, a truckload of ever so handsome fellows with lights flashing and sirens blowing pulled up. "Much ado about nothing," I thought. They had called the gas company but told them that they would check it out first, so I watched as they took apart the offending noisemakers and used meters to check the gas lines and furnace.

Again, as sudden as it had started, it ended. They were sure that *all* my detectors were faulty even though they were brand new, 10-year detectors. As they were walking out the door, the alarms began chirping again, even the alarm system chimed in, and they joked that it was a poltergeist. They left nonetheless.

Back at my desk, I called my friend to tell her what was going on when the doorbell rang. It was the gas company. I told them the fire department couldn't find anything, but they insisted on checking everything out anyway. I headed back to my desk to continue my phone call when I noticed a man in the backyard, waving at his partner and a sudden flurry of activity.

One man ran around front; the other was on the phone calling someone then running back and forth, only this time to my back door. "Ma'am, do you have any candles burning?" he asked through his winded breath. I responded with a confused, "no." He replied, "You have a gas leak!"

My mouth dropped. My dream was a warning. The pipe outside was rusted on top where snow perches itself during our long winters. The winds were sporadically blowing the gas into the house through the very space around the pipe. The only thing that saved me from disaster were those stark, strong winds and my profoundly accurate dream.

Your dreams and intuition are always speaking, and many times, we forego the obvious because it seems too easy. We dismiss the simple and natural ways information comes in lieu of a dog and pony show. The greatest teacher, the greatest prophet, lives in you.

Messages in dreams or clairaudience, the ability to hear messages, are far more common than you think. But many simply ignore them or become frightened, thinking they are losing their mind. They reveal past lives and play scenes from previous incarnations and often foretell the future which most dismiss.

I was dining with a new client and her husband. She was skeptical even though she had signed both up for six weeks of classes. We dined at a lovely atrium, where the dessert was a round or two of karaoke. She was a fan of my singing and excited to show off her own voice. We planned to be out that Friday evening until at least ten o'clock.

We'd just barely ordered when something I am used to, but most would be mortified by began occurring. My left brain was arguing with Spirit in my own head; it was a battle of wills. I was saying, "No! I can't say that!" but Spirit practically hounded me, "Now, you must say it now!"

Suddenly, without any warning, like a ball of fire shooting from a window, these words flew out of my mouth: "Your daughter is about to take her own life! But we have time to fix this!"

The battle inside my head continued, one side saying, "She's going to hate me!" The other side was more appeasing; "You are in service to humanity, no matter what the cost to your personal life or friendships."

An awkward and eerie silence fell over the room, and no one moved. The look of shock on her face told me I'd just shot myself in the foot, so long to my new client and friend. We had only been at the Atrium restaurant for about forty minutes when she suddenly bolted from the table. With a hasty apology and goodbye, she and her husband were gone. My chest sank. I left, resigned that I would never hear from them again, two people I'd grown to care about in a very short time. As I drove away, I saw Amanda dialing her phone looking frantic and watched as their car faded into traffic.

That night I could not sleep. I could feel Amanda and her daughter interlocked in a battle for life. The next morning, I called their business. Martin, Amanda's husband, answered the phone.

"Does she hate me?" I asked.

His reply surprised me. "I don't know. Let me ask her... Amanda, Ariaa wants to know if you hate her?"

A shrill voice in the distance shouted, "*Hate her? No!* Tell her she's a blessing! I will call her in a minute!"

Within minutes, she phoned and started rambling so fast it was hard to hear what she was saying. After a round of overflowing gratitude and gushing accolades, she told me that at the very moment I'd told her that her daughter was going to attempt to take her own life, the twenty-year-old was sitting in the closed garage with the car running. She had planned it. She left her five-year-old daughter with her grandparents for the weekend and told them she was going with friends to the mountains. As she sat in the car, the garage filling with carbon monoxide, she was writing goodbye letters to her mom and daughter. When her mother left the restaurant and called her on the drive home, she later said that she knew it was God stopping her.

I was recently dining at a Mediterranean restaurant with another couple who I've known for several years. I've counseled his wife off and on, and we became friends in the process. He'd recently brought one of my books and was spiritually awakening. As we sat dining and laughing through small banter and a well-seasoned belly-dancer bumping to the rhythms of music from the East, the talk led to places we would like to travel. Without skipping a beat, I turned to him and said, "You should go to Spain. You knew the great

Ponce de Leon!" Now, mind you, I knew little to nothing of this man—not Ponce de Leon or my client's husband—but his face said it all.

He launched into a tale of his father, a master saddle maker. He had worked alongside his dad for years mastering the craft which brought his dad so much joy. He continued his story and revealed that several years earlier, his father had been commissioned to repair the saddle of none other than Ponce de Leon. He traveled with his dad on that special assignment and had handled and repaired this rare saddle, of the man he knew in decades gone by. There is always validation, and every moment of insight is critical in attuning to and connecting with your past. Trusting your gut feeling, listening to the voice within you, and acting in a timely fashion on whatever you're being guided to do, wherever you are being guided to go, contributes greatly to surfacing your past lives.

Now, as I sat before this meager, pumpkin-haired client, I wondered what was about to unfold. I led him into a deep meditation where surrender occurs and emotions are moot. It is when in an altered state that the authentic aspects of your soul are unleashed. Looking through the lens of a seer, I was instantly enthralled. A familiar face began to morph over his, replete with curly red locks and a perfectly positioned beret. Now, mind you, I had on a few occasions been to the Louvre in Paris, and this ancient face before me looked oddly familiar to some I had seen in that art gallery. But I couldn't quite place it.

I whispered to the heavens, "Who is that?"

A distinct and familiar voice loudly resounded in my ears. "Ariaa, he's Rembrandt."

I scrambled to mute the microphone and immediately Googled images of the art master, hoping to find a few validating ones, which matched. To my astonishment, there he was, portrayed exactly as I was seeing him with Rembrandt's image morphed over his face. Once again, there was that uncanny, modern-day resemblance I've been witness to so many times over the years with others I've taught. It always amazes me how much the facial features carry over into subsequent lifetimes. The resemblance remains, particularly in predominate lives where there was great success or a strong identity to the character they embodied. The irony is always icing on the proverbial cake; my client recently had an overwhelming desire to paint and even thought about buying some art supplies and taking a class.

I hesitated to tell him what I'd seen since he was coming out of an altered state of meditation, and I was unsure if he would think I was completely nuts. Becoming aware of some of your more predominant lifetimes is a double-edged sword for two reasons; it can cause arrogance to rise, and some might try to duplicate or even capitalize on their former fame or other aspects of that life. Or, it can bring up great disappointment in what you've chosen this time around, especially if your life today is unremarkable or ordinary.

I once told a twenty-five-year-old client of a lifetime of great notoriety, which sadly turned him into a gloating goat, taunting and lauding it over everyone. Humble lifetimes are a gift for so many reasons. In the heavenly realm, success is not measured by public fame or wealth. It is typically the small acts of kindness and love shown to total strangers, which attracts a greater sum of light and develops a higher level of consciousness.

Many people wonder, "If he was Rembrandt, then why would he choose a more discreet life this time around?" Or, "If she was a queen, then why would she live so modestly today?" Just because you've been rich in one lifetime does not mean it will reoccur time and time again. Just because you've been famous or accomplished does not mean you won't choose the opposite in subsequent lifetimes. Just because you were powerful 100 years ago does not mean you won't be obsequious today. Running the gambit of diverse experiences is an attribute in reincarnation and contributes to evolving the soul, creatively, spiritually, and intellectually.

The majority of the times, souls choose what "type" of existence they wish to experience, while a few choose randomly. If you want to acquire or enhance humility, you might choose a simpler, more obscure life. If you want to be famous, you will pick a family that enables and furthers your talents. Someone wishing to master unconditional love may choose an abusive father or mother. When you can learn to love the most unlovable human being, you accomplish the goal.

The personality may change as it develops from lifetime to lifetime, but it is the consciousness that holds all the memories and imprints. Those are seeded in such a way that often, the memory is so deeply embedded it won't re-appear until you are triggered by something external.

My friend and I often joke about how lightly we sleep. The faint sound of a hooting owl a mile away, a plane flying too low, or thunder in the distance will cause both of us to sit straight up in the bed. It stems from separate lifetimes with similar experiences where we were shocked out of sleep by something frightening. She lives in the Northwest and I in the middle of the United States, and yet our lives parallel each other's. We are twin souls, basically opposite halves of each other. What happens to her typically happens to me in today's world. In other lifetimes, we also parallel each other's experiences, and, like twin souls, we do not always return together. We have similar traits today as in many of those previous existences. There are always some, if not many, similar characteristics from one existence to another.

Rembrandt painted innumerable images of himself; today, my former client continues the tradition, in an unapologetic endless stream of selfies as he travels throughout the world, something the great Dutch master longed for but never achieved. Rembrandt was an artist, an awkward yet eccentric man and continues to be today, his personality remaining very much the same. Every time I look at the places this young man visits, I see Rembrandt. The resemblance is truly uncanny and, at times, a wee bit off-putting. Today, he does not remember or give much credence to believing that Rembrandt was one of his past lives. That typically occurs in a soul who has mastered a previous life and doesn't feel the need to revisit it, or to a soul who has had many lifetimes where skepticism played an important role. It is a characteristic that also presents when a soul finds it too painful to remember such a poignant lifetime, often wanting but unable to return to the past.

"Rembrandt" remains a friend, who I have the pleasure of watching in social media as he continues to resemble his former personality in everything he does. He no longer resonates to the strokes of paint but instead has taken up a worldlier role this time around. Rembrandt was eccentric and always wore a billowing cap or perfectly fashioned beret. Today, as an activist for the Earth's climate crisis and an entrepreneur, he's replaced the beret with a quirky, fuzzy, arctic polar bear cap, complete with long, dangling paws. Few men could pull off such an eccentric chapeau, but imprints and cellular memories, even if unawake, linger.

Chapter 4

Soul Kind

When in the presence of the "Thronal" energies, the greater sum that many call God, you have knowledge minus the human element of doubt. In such a peaceful, ethereal place, there is only pure love, pure joy, and pure wisdom or information. What is absent are human frailties and the ego, byproducts of humanness. These are doubt, sorrow, sadness, longing, regret, judgment, fear, jealousy, envy, self-loathing, and all the lower emotions exclusive to the human ego. Additionally, you instantly know the measure of all your lifetimes and those which truly had an impact on your country, the world, or history. The more mundane or ordinary lifetimes serve a purpose too, but the leadership lifetimes, where light or darkness was the predominant role, tend to have a greater impact on the soul.

Heaven, for lack of a better word, is a busy, working environment. Without Earth's gravity and a human body, it is your consciousness which carries you into other worlds and works. Like a Master Class, you can continue to learn from the great artists, teachers, philosophers, and scientists who dwell in spirit via a living hologram, or you can move directly into service, assisting in answering the prayers of those on Earth. The choice is up to you.

There is no calendar or clock marking time or urgency; in fact, there isn't any urgency at all. Spatial atmosphere is energy, frequency, vibration, color, sound, and consciousness; it is an extension of the infinite intelligence or Divine mind, what most call God.

There are souls who leave the Earth without any belief in heaven or God, therefore rarely venture to the higher, more evolved paradigms. They limit their own ability to soar higher via the constraints of a closed mind. They prevent their soul from seeing into worlds which exist only for those who are willing to explore with an open mind. You can't see what you don't believe in. Conversely, you do see what you have fashioned in your mind as truth. If you are black and want to see a black Jesus, it's done; if you are someone expecting pearly gates and Gabriel blowing his horn, that's what you will see; if you are an atheist and believe in nothing, you will see exactly that...nothingness. Your thoughts produce form.

Some atheists today had previous lifetimes where they were priests or clergy, monks or prophets, or people of faith. Past life religious persecution often produces modern-day atheists and those who are agnostic, just like being enslaved in a previous incarnation often produces modern-day racists. When a modern-day atheist dies, they instantly connect with their more evolved personas or aspects, leading them to higher plateaus where there is only one belief: that love is the timeless constant in all living creation. Seldom, if ever, does a soul subscribe to one belief system or one philosophy from lifetime to lifetime. Typically, you are encouraged by sages and guides to explore a variety of beliefs and cultures for the sake of growth and evolution.

Typically, the older the soul, the greater number of incarnations; however, that is not always the case. The term implies that there are "new souls," which is incorrect. There are souls who chose to incarnate fewer times on Earth, so often they are like babies when they arrive here. They lack the experience of navigating the vast array of emotions which accompany the human incarnation and are initially karma-free, until they create both negative and positive karma in at least one lifetime.

There are souls who inhabited pre-biblical civilizations such as Atlantis, Lemuria, and Mu. They are categorized as "the original family of God" since they are the ancient explorers who were first to tackle human incarnation. These are comprised of many of the characters in the Old and New Testaments of the Bible and other ancient texts. Many of those featured in the Bible were real, led ordinary lives, and often had extraordinary experiences. Many of them are not mythical as some have said over the years. Their lives were "experimental," and in the beginning, their gifts and abilities were far more evolved because of ignorance. For example, if you do not know that the human body has an age limit, you don't age. Thus, many of the original patriarchs lived to be what is considered today, an impossible feat—with some living as old as 950 years.

In some of those civilizations, humans could swim under water without drowning, and advanced science was predominant in other civilizations such as Atlantis. It is said that Atlantis fell because technology exceeded humanity, which retarded spiritual evolution. Suffice to say, today it isn't ignorance that enhances and enables the extraordinary; it is specificity and intention that generate manifestation.

The mind and the perceptions you form are the building blocks of all you create and generate. While ignorance may have once been bliss, today, you have scientific proof that the brain and your thoughts generate a response. Again, everything is energy. The amount of power that lies within every single awakened human being often goes unexplored. It is said that if we could harness the power within, every person on Earth would have never-ending nirvana. Those who are sleeping spiritually will continue to believe they are victims to every circumstance they deem contributes to their unhappiness. But those who are awake and aware are those who change the world. As humankind, when we reach collective mass— in other words, when enough souls harness and collectively utilize the power within—we will shift the paradigm and peace will be restored.

Your reality always matches your frequency and vice versa. When focused on sickness or disease, you become sick and you draw sick and diseased people into your world; when focused on lack or financial troubles, you attract more poverty. Whatever you focus on, the exact match will appear, which is precisely the reason so many people continue to attract the "wrong mate." Of course, there are other contributing factors to that equation, including but not limited to how much fear fuels each scenario.

In my book *Ariaaisms Spiritual Food for the Soul*, I told the story of Christopher Reeve, the actor who played Superman and star of stage, television, and movies. Prior to his "accident," he studied for the role of Dempsey Cain in the movie *Above Suspicion*. It is a 1995 American made-for-television thriller-drama film starring Christopher Reeve, Joe Mantegna, and Kim Cattrall. Christopher Reeve starred as a paralyzed police officer who plots to murder his unfaithful wife. In preparation to play the role, he did research at a rehabilitation hospital in Van Nuys and learned how to use a wheelchair to get in and out of cars. In an interview, he told the reporter how he laid with sandbags on his legs so he could "feel" what it was like to be paralyzed. On May 27, 1995, six days after the film's theatrical release, Reeve broke his neck when a horse threw him, leaving him paralyzed for the rest of his life.

Energy is creation and creation is energy. We simply attract what we focus on. After you die and leave the Earth, you view life from the higher paradigms and realize how many more solutions were available to you. All the trials and problems you encountered while on Earth suddenly look simple and solvable. Many souls learn that had they meditated regularly, had they have been more deliberate in all areas of life, they would have altered and or avoided some of the pitfalls. Every path known to humankind comes with challenges; after all, you are in life's greatest university while here on Earth. Some of your greatest challenges are those which offer the greatest rewards and catapult you to greater mastery.

There are distinguishing precepts for all souls returning to Earth. Souls evaluate the timing of their return and take the following into consideration:

- Karma; what karma has been incurred and how much you are willing to repay or postpone until another lifetime. The caveat is that the longer you take to address or repay your negative karma, the greater it grows.
- Life lessons; what you'd like to learn or master, and there is a difference. You might want to learn to play the piano or how to practice law. You might choose to master anger, judgment, or unconditional love.
- Career; choices and areas of interest you would like to explore such as music, arts, science, archeology, history, etc.
- Divine purpose; what you would like to fulfill while on the Earth. What will your legacy be?

If you wish, you are shown your many lifetimes in holographic form; what has been accomplished, what negative karma has been incurred, what positive karma has been generated, what soul group you are aligned to, what family to choose in order to garner the greatest results from all the above, and approximately how long you feel it will take for you to accomplish your goals.

And that brings me to another point: almost every person, with rare exception, knows approximately how long they are going to live. Whether it's a feeling or random thought or through deliberate conscious awareness, we all know about how long we will be on Earth. Many who want to live to be 100 years old will make it to that seasoned age, but more likely, encountered challenges in life that shorten the life span by just a few years. Many souls also die near, before, or right after their birthday. Time is linear, and most can gauge their personal life duration.

The notion that you are on your own is unfounded; everyone, without exception, has guidance. There are angels and guides for even the most unevolved souls, but typically those souls are oblivious to their presence. Guidance is always available, but you have to invoke or make your intention known, at the very least, before that help will actually come. The angels and heavenly bodies think you realize that you are god and one with the source of all, so it is incumbent upon you to ask for what you need.

It is up to you to activate what is already available to you when you command with love, not with force. In other words, it's all here now. The minute you come from a place of certainty, faith, knowing, the science of materializing, etc., everything you need enters your reality. Frequency plays a key role to manifestation; the higher your frequency, the quicker the manifestation.

Earth is a free-will zone, and nothing can be "done unto" you unless you consciously, subconsciously, or indirectly allow it.

Conversely, nothing will be done *for* you unless your thoughts invoke it or your prayers call it into action. Everything is energy, and how you wield that energy determines the outcome. Thoughts and prayers are actually the same in many ways. They are living intention, energetic projectiles. Thoughts, while often random, still create at the speed of your intentions. Prayers are a combination of faith, hope, and the movement of energy scored. They create by the measure of your faith or knowing, but if you are not a person of faith or belief, energy will still take form according to your thoughts and fears. Both generate a reaction from the universe.

So, why haven't you won the lottery, you ask? Money is a thing, not an attribute. It is an object and a tool, and thus has no value in and of itself. The belief in a monetary system is what gives paper currency value. The consciousness of poverty or lack is an attribute, a catalyst to overcome or from which to grow. The consciousness of greed or materialism is an attribute and, again, a teacher. But money is energy and nothing more, a tool to navigate the markets of Earth. "Money only makes you more of what you already are." Giving power to paper or metal (coins), and now bitcoin, is absurd when you really think about it, but humans do it every day. Money is energy and nothing more, and it is exclusive to the Earth, your temporary home. Money is used solely for the purpose of navigating this planet. It has no power in and of itself. There are enormous lessons to be gained with all dynamics surrounding money and the usage of it.

You didn't arrive on the most beautiful of all planets to procure, though society has conditioned you to believe that having and getting "stuff" is a large part of your existence. You came here to give, to share, to grow, to learn, to heal, to integrate, to master, and to rise. Having a "get" mentality is about as low on the frequency spectrum as you can get. Money does not create a life but is essential to survival, so it must be viewed and treated as energy. How you perceive, treat, and wield money determines the role money will play in your life.

Giving and serving are the elements which take you into the world of plenty, because there is a constant stream of goodness that encircles and returns to a giver. The giver's well is never empty and will never know a drought. Giving is the ultimate prosperity because it ensures a steady return.

Chapter 5

The Fame Game

I am often asked if everyone has a famous life. The answer is no; however, let's first define fame by 21st century standards. *Webster's Dictionary* defines fame as: "the state of being known or talked about by many people, especially on account of notable achievements; known to the general public." Before social media and television, before newspapers and information highways, people rose to fame but never made the history books, and few were recorded by scribes.

An example would be the man who ran into the Temples of Alexandra when they were being burned to the ground for the last time. He saved what we now know as the Dead Sea Scrolls. Or, let's look at the three women, who have been unknown to the majority of Americans for more than 60 years but recently gained a modicum of fame with the release of a movie about their lives.

Hidden Figures chronicled the lives of Katherine G. Johnson, Dorothy Vaughan, and Mary Jackson, African American women working at NASA, who served as the brains behind the space launch of astronaut John Glenn and those who followed. If not for that movie, released in 2016, few would know about their incredible achievements. In 2015, Barack Obama awarded Johnson the Presidential Medal of Freedom. In November 2019, she was selected to receive to the Congressional Gold Medal, the highest honor presented by Congress to a civilian. Dorothy Vaughan and Mary Jackson were posthumously awarded Congressional Gold Medals, also in 2019. Creola Katherine Johnson, whose calculations of orbital mechanics as a NASA employee were critical to the success of the first and subsequent spaceflights, passed away in 2020 at the ripe and fulfilled age of 101.

There are so many more people worldwide who have done remarkable things yet never became famous for their accomplishments. Fame, for all the good it can do in reaching millions of people worldwide, can also be a demonstrative beast and has been the source of embarrassment for many in the secular and spiritual communities.

After her spiritual awakening, actress and author Shirley MacLaine was ostracized by many in the film community and by some in her own family. After a "reading," famed journalist Barbara Walters and James Van Praagh, the noted medium, went head-to-head over information about her health because a doctor and clinical tests disputed what Praagh had predicted. He retorted with an excuse that only added to the media fervor. Noted author James Twyman battled internet trolls, aka haters, in social media long before it became a daily occurrence for anyone deemed threatening and for trolls, that usually means everyone.

A host of psychics, mediums, spiritual mystics, and others who are gifted often find themselves targeted by those who fear what they don't understand. Many have been baited, mocked, and labeled on national talk shows, in newspaper articles, and in YouTube videos, and several have become more reclusive over the years as a result. Fame, for anyone who is different than what society deems "normal," is a double-edged sword. Most of us who do this work or who've been offered fame have deliberately avoided its blade over the years.

Souls don't choose fame. They may seek it, but that is not typically in the outline they co-write for themselves before entering Earth. Fame is a derivative of energy, a byproduct. The more powerful lifetimes a soul has, in most cases, the more energy and quantified light they embody. Additionally, the more powerful the soul, the more they are able to control fame or anonymity. While quantified energy can contribute to fame, it does not necessarily mean a soul with previous powerful incarnations will automatically be famous the next time around.

Conversely, fame can also be attributed to an under-developed soul. The less one knows or has experienced as a soul, the more they may be propelled to chase shiny objects, like the lure of stardom. Once you are incarnate on the Earth, choosing fame for the sake of fame is often relegated to lesser evolved souls. There will always be those who hunger for attention, especially negative attention. Stardom for the sake of fame often leads to unsavory habits, attracting usury, and indulging in excess, like drugs or alcohol often leaving a soul empty and unfulfilled. We've witnessed the premature end of so many lives, stars who caught the wave of fame only to drown in its accoutrement.

Additionally, some souls who choose neither are often lifted to the heights of fame via good karma for purposes of service, inspiration, or as a tool to teach others or themselves. Susan Boyle, the Scottish singer who became a global sensation in 2009, is one such soul. Her meteoric rise to fame and fortune after appearing on *Britain's Got Talent* was, for her, wonderful, and yet became a heavy cross as time went by. She once told reporters that she would give it all up to have her anonymity back and, to some degree, she has regained it over the last 12 years. Fame often shows up in soul groups like the Windsor and Kennedy families, who have returned time and time again together. Their collective energy and sadly, their collective karma, positive and negative, are the reason and cause of their many tragedies and successes. These souls often become so alike in energy that their actions are in synchronicity in every area of their lives, from the personal to the professional. The dynamics of a tight soul group often produce fame, fortune—and often accomplish a great deal more, kind of like the old saying, "Two heads are better than one." However, concentrated energy is always accompanied by attached karma, both individually and collectively. Every soul group which returns together repeatedly is subject to the karma as a whole.

Suffice to say, what you choose is up to you, and all of it can be redirected at any given point in your Earth awakening. You can diminish negative karma, increase positive karma, and you can even lengthen the number of years you are on the Earth. You have all the power you need once you tune into the higher, non-emotional self. Altered states such as meditation or hypnosis are the best way to access a higher perspective. There are many advantages to developing the higher self which are waiting to be employed.

The wisest souls learn from the most difficult lifetimes. If you choose a hearing or seeing impaired life, you learn to use all your other senses and they become more heightened. The next time you return to Earth, those senses will be sharper and more perceptive. It is perception, tenacity, and perseverance which determine the quality of each choice and how much you derive from the challenges each lifetime offers.

There are so many choices to experience when returning to Earth. Typically, you choose gender, explore what purpose you are going to fulfill, and you decide approximately how many years it will take for you to accomplish what you have chosen. Without taking the time to address and amend for the past life karma, people feel like victims to their own karmic return. That is how important past lives are. Karma always finds its way back to the sender. When you become aware of negative karma, doing the work to clear, heal, and forgive yourself, releases, diminishes, or dissolves the energy. You often decide what karma you are willing to repay (recognizing that the longer you postpone karma the greater it grows), which lessons you wish to engage, and then you choose a family that will accommodate what you've selected. The goal is always to continue up the ladder, so to speak. You want to increase and sustain the highest frequency available, and hopefully you will never digress, but you won't remember any of that once you arrive on Earth.

What determines if you come back into a family of familiar souls or souls with which you have not had previous lifetimes? There are many reasons to continue returning together, and much of it is related to karma and completing lessons. There are also great opportunities to explore with those you have never encountered before. What you do to another, whether intentional or not, returns to you in some way or fashion. Earth is already challenging enough, so returning with familiar souls or aligning to your core soul group is natural. Conversely, returning to Earth in an unfamiliar soul group offers diverse and extraordinary experiences that the comfort of familiarity denies.

Some souls choose opposite polarities to gain an expansive perspective of what Earth depicts as heaven and hell, while others choose to dabble in the occult or even atheism. Earth is the ultimate university, and with so many options to choose from, most souls will run the gambit from one extreme scenario to another. Great souls are rarely produced from mundane lifetimes. The more challenges and hurdles you overcome, integrate, then evolve from, the more likely you will arrive at the ultimate destination, which is becoming self-aware and self-realized.

Suffering is not a necessary element to the soul's evolution, but experiencing different cultures, beliefs, family dynamics, diverse locations, and everything from living in a healthy body to living in one that betrays you, creates character and foundational elements like resilience. Resilience and tenacity are essential to spiritual evolution and developing consciousness. Balance is also foundational in choosing to return to planet Earth.

If a soul chooses too many dark lives, the karma builds and the nature of darkness sets into the soul, often making basic things like telling the truth a challenge. Feeding the darkness in previous lifetimes, which many choose to experience for a variety of reasons, is often hard to look at in today's light. Killing, rape, torture, theft, and cruelty, emotional or physical, can have lasting effects on the soul and its karma. Intention plays an instrumental role in how strong the karma is upon its return, whether in the same lifetime or in subsequent lifetimes. It is a fact that what you put out *will* return to you, whether it is rooted in love or stems from hate. Conversely, if a soul chooses many consecutive lifetimes in the light or in service to the light, the opposite happens. The more you engage in serving others, the greater you expand your consciousness, and you automatically begin to hunger for a deeper level of serving.

Goodness begets more goodness; hate begets more hate. The greater nobility, humility, altruistic acts, and genuine good you put into the world, the more the world rewards you energetically and the more good karma follows you. The smallest acts of kindness are significant and count, such as rescuing a dog that's about to cross the road or feeding squirrels and birds. In fact, many times, it is the smaller acts of good which have a domino effect on others and become a contagion, that make the most difference in the world.

All roads lead to the same heaven. It is karma that differentiates how clear your vision is once you arrive.

Chapter 6

Continuity

There are souls who return to continue the work they began in previous lifetimes, and often, there are telltale signs of who they've previously been.

Abraham Lincoln is one of such souls. He began the ardent task of freeing black Americans from slavery but was assassinated before the job was done. Sixty-four years later, he returned as a black man born in 1929, knowing that when he reached manhood, he would lead America and usher in the civils rights movement. As Lincoln, he left an indelible mark on history and accomplished what he came to do. As Martin Luther King, Jr., he was able to continue his fight for the black man's freedom as a black man.

There is a black and white news video in existence, though hard to find, of Dr. Martin Luther King, Jr. waiting to be introduced by Ralph David Abernathy, to deliver his last and most famous "I've been to the mountaintop" speech at Mason Temple, April 3, 1968, on the eve of his assassination. In an article written by Joseph Rosenbloom for *The Guardian*, Rev.

Billy Kyles, pastor of Mason Temple church and friend of Dr. King, spoke about that night and the storm which kept people waiting for more than an hour and a half for Dr. King to arrive. "Time and again, wind gusts punched open two large window fans near the ceiling of the auditorium. The shutters clacked shut each time, startling King." "Every time there was a bang," Billy Kyles recalled later, "he would flinch."

Dr. King knew his time on Earth was coming to an end. The profound speech which followed was further evidence. When you compare the way both men died, you'll find the cellular imprint or memory of his previous assassination was strong enough that it caused a repeat incident. King died the exact same way he did when he was Lincoln, by assassination. King was shot on the right side of his head—technically, his jaw— while Lincoln was shot on the left side of his head. Though location isn't essential to the scenario, it speaks to cellular memory.

The famous Country Western star, Patsy Cline, who recorded such hits as "Crazy" and "I Fall to Pieces," died at the age of 30, in a tragic plane crash on March 5, 1963. Gone too soon, it is widely known that she had ominously foreseen her own demise. Apparently, this talented woman was not finished with her life as a country singer, because nineteen years later, she returned as a famous country crossover singer today. She is every bit as successful in her new incarnation as she was in her old one, but she made some changes while in heaven. She went from having black hair to blonde, from stocky to wafer-thin, and from straight, country western music to including other genres in her current day repertoire. Like most souls, hers decided to evolve and be able to cross over, ensuring she would be just as successful this time around. This time, she will live to accomplish her dreams and achieve that which was unfinished when she left the Earth as Patsy Cline, prematurely.

I recently connected with her on social media and told her what I knew, that she indeed had been Patsy. I waited twenty years to convey this valuable piece of the puzzle to her and was relieved when she replied:

"Yes there has always been a strong pull and understanding there. It's been quite eerie."

I can't tell you how relieved I was. I didn't even realize how much lighter I would feel after expelling the revelation. As an instrument, I feel a certain responsibility to be a good steward of these gifts. I was not surprised that she knew her own past, but still feel assured that she will walk with a different posture now that she knows that someone else knows, too.

Not all souls return to finish previous works. Many choose lives that are polar opposite from the previous one. From poor to rich or religious to atheist, creative to technical, there are so many polarities to explore. With rare exception, souls love to grow, evolve, learn, and teach. The most certain way to die is to stop growing. All souls are teachers, even if in the most negative of ways. All souls have purpose and benefit someone, somewhere, even if they are unaware of it. Returning to Earth is a natural progression to further the path of learning.

Even great sages have returned in many lifetimes to evolve and continue to share eternal wisdom. You may be sitting at Starbucks right now next to a once renowned author, artist, scientist, philosopher, or Biblical or historical character. That is a lovely thought, isn't it? Sadly, you probably missed it because you were looking at your phone or device and never looked up or acknowledged them. A nod, a smile, a hello to a stranger keeps the world connected.

Because people cannot see past lives in those they interact with every day, it is just plain common sense to give attention equally to all people from all walks of life. Think of it as a catalyst to be kinder, gentler, and more attentive to those around you. There is no need to be impressed, but how fascinating to know that you are interacting with history and those who've made a real difference in history, every single day. You may also be interacting with those who have destroyed or taken life, those who have been dangerous and may still be today. All souls return no matter who or what they've been before.

No human is more important than any other and all roles are essential to the greater fabric of life. What matters is to recognize that living history is walking among you every day and, hopefully, you embrace the notion that we learn greatly from every soul on the planet. You could be in the presence of greatness when passing that homeless man by. You could be sitting next to Marie Curie at the DMV or listening to John Lennon on Spotify, in that new artist everyone loves. Your child with a flair for art might just be Monet or Michelangelo. Every soul created has had significant lifetimes, and while they may not remember specifically who they were, suffice to say many of their gifts remain and very well may accompany them into their new incarnation.

Over the years, I've been host to many who lived during the Second World War, and their memories are typically stark and traumatizing after more than 75 years. One client vividly recalls being starved to death at the Nazi death camp in Auschwitz-Birkenau, Poland, where more than one million human beings died. She returned today as a massage therapist and healer, working with essential oils to help relieve pain and stress in her clients. She was born with deformed feet, from the memory or imprint of arthritis and atrophy brought on by the bitter cold and exposure, slow starvation, and the brutal labor women and men were subject to.

Many people today do not realize they are suffering from past life PTSD, post-traumatic stress disorder. You can be perfectly healthy, incredibly intelligent, and suddenly begin to have panic attacks or fear for no obvious reason. You can suddenly manifest psoriasis, acne, or a sudden onset allergy without knowing why. People who have never smoked cigarettes today are suddenly diagnosed with lung cancer. Women I've counseled often speak of feeling safe and secure, when suddenly they become frightened at bedtime, sensing that someone is standing over them. Emotional scarring runs deep, and if you were once burned at the stake, you will most likely have a fear—or, at the very least, a healthy respect for fire when you return. Rape, incest, torture, deprivation, mutilation, religious rituals such as human sacrifice, and more often set deep in the spirit and leave imprints in the cellular memory. As you grow and experience life, some of these will show up, giving you an opportunity to heal the memory. Miscarriages are connected to past life loss because with rare exception, almost every female in history has experienced the loss of a child or fetus.

Nearly 100 percent of all souls return to Earth to finish, heal, or continue what they began in another lifetime—and not necessarily in the most immediate past life. Like taking a gap year before attending college, some souls wait until the time is right to return, while others come back immediately. The risk of a speedy return is that you may imprint your previous life's emotional or physical damage into your newborn body. Cellular memory includes both, and often, staying out of body and on the other side for an extended period of time helps you understand and heal the damage done before returning to Earth.

You also may return swiftly to Earth, only to find that connections with your previous family members have changed and they will. The dynamic continues to grow with every crossing and every return. Even your feelings for certain people you've previously incarnated and interacted with will change. One of the reasons many don't have a memory of their immediate past life is they would find it too painful to return. If you were madly in love, died prematurely, then returned in a short time, the feelings would be on another level.

As I mentioned earlier, I had a conversation with Jenny Cockell, who was previously Mary Sutton, an Irish woman who died in 1932. Jenny Cockell was born in 1953. Having connected with Jenny on Facebook, I wanted to know if the emotions she felt about and for her children were different this time around. Did she feel as connected to the now senior citizens, her previous children, as she had when she was Mary Sutton, their mother? She admitted that there was a sort of disconnect with a few of them, and it was different, but the core love and feeling of family was intact. She went on to say that she had changed even though her early life was spent trying to find her previous children. For her, the key was to discover if they were okay, and once she found them and knew they'd all had relatively good lives, she was contented. She has evolved into a more scientific mind and personality this time around, so naturally, her emotional levels are much more subdued. It is no surprise that her emotions would be more evolved and diverse, but again, love lives on.

There are so many variables to choose from when returning to Earth. Each one adds a different level of learning and contributes to evolving the consciousness while healing the past. With rare exception, most souls have run the gambit of living in both darkness and light. Ancient lifetimes were often brutal and Neanderthalic, producing many warriors and many martyrs. Some who once took life when they were great warriors or soldiers have now returned to Earth to preserve life as healers, doctors, nurses, or caregivers. Those who were black slaves or segregationists, if wise, typically returned as politicians and activists fighting for equality. Those who were homophobic may very well have returned to Earth gay or transgender.

I have a friend, a medical doctor, who is transgender now but lived for more than 60 years as a heterosexual. She was a husband and father for more than 30 years. With great trepidation and concern for her career and children, she transitioned in her late 60s, having the unique opportunity to explore so much more of her soul's development from both the male and female perspective.

Souls who have had more female lifetimes than male or more male lifetimes than female often struggle today to find their true identity. In her case and in transgender people, the soul knows from childhood that they are the opposite of the gender they've been born into. The choice is not made on Earth—gay, transgender, bi-sexual, and those questioning their identity are all born into their identity.

The energy from previous lives determines the energy which incarnates. If you've had 60 female lifetimes and only 40 male, but are born male today, chances are you will want to be female and romantically favor women. I've met many heterosexual men who have a strong effeminate but remain hetero. I've met some gay men who are so saturated with female energy that they are beautifully and wildly effeminate. Bi-sexual souls are probably the most evolved of all because bi-sexuality indicates an equal balance of both male and female lifetimes, and in higher paradigms or heaven, all are androgynous.

There are two essential elements to human life, and they are learning and growing; otherwise, there is no need to return to Earth. Earth holds extraordinary challenges and opportunities to evolve as both a soul and a human being. There are so many cultures to learn from, so many variables to enhance the human experience. There are still some who refuse to grow; they get stuck and never aspire beyond the simplest of human experiences. Many don't even know what they are aspiring to or for, since they don't remember what living with few, if any, limitations means.

Lifetime after lifetime, we return to search for what has always been innate; the master lives within, you are that master. While that may sound cliché, the fact is, you are far more remarkable a creation than you perceive or are willing to tap into. The reason many avoid the extraordinary is simple; one must take personal responsibility for everything that occurs in their life, from thoughts to actions to reactions. We choose in many ways, some conscious, some subconscious, some from dysfunction, and some propelled by past life memories and unfinished karma. Many people are either oblivious to previous lifetimes or the role they play today, or they don't know how to clear karma, heal the past, and integrate the strengths from previous lifetimes.

No one should be burdened by an invisible past they cannot imagine. However, when there are no obvious reasons or answers for today's dilemmas, one has to consider the past.

Chapter 7

The Alchemist

Sages from Jesus to Buddha have taught the alchemy of mastery over the physical and emotional worlds, and yet, here we are in the 21st century and we are still doing things laboriously.

The ancient prophecies refer to a time in the near future when all humankind will live in harmony with one another, for a thousand years, in peace. It is written that there will be no hate or war and that everything on Earth will be restored to its original perfection. If that is true, then humankind has a long way to go, because it often appears we are going backward. Race wars, political wars, oil wars, poverty, ignorance, and greed all play a part in the descension of consciousness and continue to plague humankind.

What exists but has yet to be found in ancient scrolls buried eons ago is that the mind or consciousness is the greatest purveyor of progress. I am not referring to planning or building. I am referring to envisioning and manifesting, using the laws and principles of quantum physics, to create the reality of plenty and peace for all.

The brain acts as a compartmentalized receptor for consciousness. While more research on the brain and its unlimited potential is necessary, most spiritualists know that whatever you achieve in the mind, you manifest in the world. Stabilizing the vision to bring it into the fore is paramount. There is no room for doubt or wonder, and an iota of either affects the outcome. In the age of technology with the potential danger of misuse and technology exceeding humanity, now is the time to employ mind over matter and hyper-focused vision. In scores of ancient and modern books, sages and teachers have long taught the principles and alchemy employed to reach through the veils to the invisible, so why have so many failed to follow their lead? The definitive way to access the invisible or to direct energy effectively begins with stripping away the veils of belief, ego, and fear. Present-day regret, emotional harboring, and unhealed cellular memories form an energy clot in the flow of higher spiritual truth, preventing the access of more evolved capabilities.

As you heal the emotional body, you heal the physical one. As you strip away all aspects of the ego, you uncover the alchemy of a walk between two worlds. The ego is the vessel of all lower emotional seeds such as, but not limited to:

- Insecurity
- Arrogance
- Jealousy
- Pride

- Self-absorption
- Sadness
- Anger
- Fear
- Shame
- Disgust
- Hate
- Grief
- Self-loathing
- Contempt
- Envy
- Vengefulness

These are the veils which prevent mastery and obscure the magic of previous lifetimes longing to seep through. Conversely, they are the tools which, when examined and explored, either polish or retard the human spirit. Those who balance these lower emotions with meditation or other spiritual practices, such as chanting, yoga, Tai Chi, or Pilates, often integrate and heal these agents of change.

It begins with questioning every aspect of you. Self-discovery is evaluating what triggers you—why something in particular makes you sad, or angry, or happy. Are you inspired by a movie, or art, or a particular travel location? The "why" of everything is the entrance ramp to self-awareness, self-sufficiency, and enlightenment. By seeking to understand yourself, you uncover not only your current life wounds, but you delve deeper into past life memories, exploring those which left a mark or imprint on your body, consciousness, and soul.

*Self-analysis is the predecessor to self-awareness,
self-awareness is the predecessor to self-realization, and
self-realization is the predecessor to the enlightened mind.*

The daily practice of meditation opens the doors to the past, present, and future and enables a less emotional or non-emotional state. Research has proven both the physical and emotional benefits of meditating regularly. Meditation is the key to transcending space and time in a non-emotional or attached way and allows you to tap into every area you deem necessary, for your own personal and spiritual growth. Additionally, meditation has profound benefits on biochemistry and the brain.

Neuroscientists recently discovered that people who meditate regularly have more gray matter in the frontal cortex, which is an area of the brain linked to decision-making and working memory. The cortex of the brain shrinks as you age, yet in one study, fifty-year-old meditators had the same amount of gray matter as those half their age.

Over the past twenty-five years, there have been hundreds of studies on the benefits of meditating, and science has concluded that the daily practice of meditating is accompanied by some or all of these benefits:

- Lowers heart rate.
- Lowers blood pressure.
- Releases stress, which is the cause of many diseases and sicknesses.

- Lowers pulse rate giving the body a chance to reacclimate.
- Increases oxygen to the brain and cells of the body, improving functionality.
- Reduces anxiety by lowering levels of blood lactate.
- Helps in post-op healing.
- Enhances the immune system.
- Decreases the aging process.
- Enhances energy, strength, and vigor.
- Helps with weight loss.
- Reduction of free radicals, less tissue damage.
- Drop in cholesterol levels, lowers risk of cardiovascular disease.
- Builds self-confidence.
- Increases serotonin level, influences mood and behavior.
- Resolves phobias and fears.
- Helps discipline own thoughts.
- Helps with focus and concentration.
- Increases creativity.
- Increases brain wave coherence.
- Improves learning ability and memory.
- Increases feelings of vitality and rejuvenation.
- Increases emotional stability.
- Mind and body age at slower rate.
- Develops intuition.
- Able to see the larger picture in a given situation.
- Increases ability to solve complex problems.
- Develops willpower.

- Greater communication between the two brain hemispheres.
- React more quickly and more effectively to a stressful event.
- Increases one's perceptual ability and motor performance.
- Higher intelligence growth rate.
- Increases job satisfaction.
- Less aggressiveness.
- Develops emotional maturity.
- Helps keep things in perspective.
- Provides peace of mind, happiness.
- Helps you discover your purpose.
- Increases self-actualization.
- Increases compassion.
- Deeper understanding of yourself and others.
- Brings body, mind, spirit in harmony.
- Increases acceptance of oneself.
- Enhances the ability to forgive.
- Changes attitude toward life.
- Helps with living in the present moment.
- Creates a widening, deepening capacity for love.
- Discover the power and consciousness beyond the ego.
- An inner sense of "assurance or knowingness."
- Increases the synchronicity in your life.

Developing a regular and consistent routine, and meditating at approximately the same time every day, further enhances these benefits.

We've seen the results of large groups of children or adults meditating together to affect a cause. I've led many large and small groups of meditations for global change, and often the results have been nothing short of miraculous. Studies have shown the effect of a large group of meditators on crime levels too. One such study in Washington, D.C. demonstrated that violent crime decreased by a rate of 23.3 percent during the experimental period from June 7 to July 30. The odds of this occurring by chance in 1993 were less than 2 in 1 billion.

Another long-term study was conducted at Princeton University by the Global Consciousness Project. They found that a large group focused on one ideal or principle generated very significant results. The changes were significant when collective attention was focused on thoughts like love or peace. "Where two or three are gathered," takes on an entirely new meaning when you understand energy and frequency. The very word "love" or "God" or "hate" is power-packed with the energy of historical usage. Collective mass is similar to mass hysteria but with deliberate and focused intention.

Meditation serves a greater purpose globally since collective consciousness is predicated on the notion that all thoughts gather, collect, and create. Meditation serves not only the receiver of the higher frequency, but it serves the greater good. In other words, you become an instrument of light that permeates the atmosphere and affects the world at large. Meditation is the way to raise the frequency of the Earth, thus raising the frequency of humankind. Higher frequency lends to peace, prosperity, and love.

Gaëlle Desbordes, a neuroscientist and instructor in radiology at Harvard Medical School, demonstrated that "changes in brain activity in subjects who have learned to meditate hold steady even when they're not meditating." That is an enormous discovery, particularly when you recognize the value and implications that meditation has, not just on individuals but on the global spectrum as well.

In 1978, 7,000 individuals came together to meditate on love and peace and embodying these powerful projectiles; they radiated and directed the energy outwardly. Over the course of three weeks, a 16 percent drop in violence and global crimes occurred. It was called the "Maharishi Effect," and even suicide rates and auto accidents were reduced during that three-week period. Additionally, a 72 percent reduction in terrorist activities occurred during this same period. The benefits of group meditation and its impact on every kind of situation has been researched and documented in more than 50 studies. The psychological effects, the physiological changes in the body, and the continued health benefits make mediation the best medicine known to humankind.

Quantum physics has proven that everything is energy, including and especially our thoughts and feelings. Every thought you have radiates into the outer field known as the "collective conscious" and is amplified by like thoughts or energy. Loving yourself and harnessing the peace and love within you through meditation can positively affect not only your personal self and reality, but the world at large. While my work and emphasis is on chakra meditation because of its powerful effects on expeditious transformation, the type of meditation you choose or create for yourself is up to you. The key to any good meditation is to lose yourself and let go of any formulated thoughts and simply allow light consumption. Within that engulfing paradigm, magic unfolds, and the problems of a human being are silenced while in this all-consuming, non-emotional state.

Many consider "consciousness" to be what we refer to as the soul and its composition of energy, memory, color, sound, and frequency. The memories within the human brain are vast and yet selective, but cellular memory presents a different challenge. When you enter Earth's atmosphere by being born as a baby, you imprint the most memorable events into the newly formed body. While most people retain at least some of their past life memories, it is typically on a subconscious level. At the conscious level, most know nothing of who they have been in previous civilizations; however, there is evidence that cellular memory is deeply embedded within every single cell in the human body.

Cellular imprint is characteristic of the most important or traumatic events a person experiences. Do I have scientific evidence? Yes and no. I have nearly three decades of case studies and experience witnessing firsthand what my clients feel, perceive, experience, and react to. Hypnosis and regression have played a key role and have also uncovered some pretty remarkable memories in many of those I've served.

In his book *Return to Life-Extraordinary Cases of Children Who Remember Past Lives*, Dr. Jim Tucker, Professor of

Psychiatry and Neurobehavioral Science at the University of Virginia, chronicled his case studies of more than 2,500 children who reported memories of past lives. Some of the stories exhibited traits and features of which reincarnation was the singular explanation.

The most respected and best known of those who have collected data that appears to provide scientific proof that reincarnation is real—is the life's work of Dr. Ian Stevenson. He authored several books, including *Where Reincarnation and* Biology *Intersect* and *Children Who Remember Previous Lives.* In his 40 years of research, Dr. Stevenson devoted his life to scientific documentation of past life memories of children from all over the world. Having studied more than three thousand cases, he is considered the leading authority in reincarnation studies.

You cannot broach this subject without mentioning Dr. Brian Weiss, a Yale-educated psychiatrist and leading regressionist of past life therapy. I became aware of Brian more than twenty-eight years ago, right after my own profound experience in the Alps of Austria. We met a few months later, and I was struck by how astute and knowledgeable he was, considering he did not believe in reincarnation before 1980. In his book *Many Lives, Many Masters: The True Story of a Prominent Psychiatrist, His Young Patient, and the Past-Life Therapy That Changed Both Their Lives,* he tells the story of his patient Catherine, who began sharing details of one of her past lives under hypnosis. He has gone on to lecture all over the world, has regressed more than 8,000 patients, and has written a host of books on the subject. He is considered one of the most knowledgeable and convincing experts on reincarnation.

Ruth Montgomery, Arthur Ford, Edgar Cayce, and so many others have written a host of books on the subject. However, some of the greatest minds in history have also written or spoken about this once controversial topic. Voltaire, Ralph Waldo Emerson, Benjamin Franklin, Leo Tolstoy, Blavatsky, Friedrich Nietzsche, Henry Ford, and even Socrates all believed in reincarnation.

The Zohar text from the Kaballah says, "The souls must reenter the absolute substance whence they have emerged. But to accomplish this, they must develop all the perfections, the germ of which is planted in them; and if they have not fulfilled this condition during one life, they must commence another, a third, and so forth, until they have acquired the condition which fits them for reunion with God."

Whenever there is an awakening to a past life, there is an initial shock that comes with learning of those you have previously been, particularly when your actions or intentions were harmful. What most don't understand is that your previous lives and experiences have either taught you what not to be, or they have made you more of what you are. You cannot judge your actions from hundreds, even thousands of years ago, by who you are today. That has been a point of contention with many who have awakened to some of their previous incarnations.

People often get caught up in the shock, horror, or guilt of something they've done or experienced in a previous life. Many have a very difficult time overcoming the notion that they have ever done anything to harm another. Yet, often upon learning the circumstances or details of previous lifetimes, greater insight into their psyche at the time emerges. Removing any judgment you feel toward yourself or others who were involved is key to healing the past. It's easy to tell who you've shared lifetimes with most of the time; you will love them instantly, loathe them for no apparent reason, or feel flat-lined and neutral about them.

Those who played critical roles in your previous lifetimes might create friction, remorse, and a host of other emotions, including immense love. The purpose for coming back together is calibrated by energy and occurs to give you the opportunity to reveal and heal, and thus move forward. Letting go of things you've harbored for many lifetimes is not only soul liberating, it also frees the body from detrimental imprints which can cause sickness and dis-ease, if allowed to fester.

Hopefully, today you are more evolved, educated, and enlightened. Hopefully, you have worked your way up the karmic scale, resolving some of the negative energy you put into the world previously. The majority of souls do heal their past life damage and traumas, since Earth is the ultimate university. But there are handfuls of souls who perpetuate their darker lives because they either enjoy it or have not found a way to escape the hold the darkness has over them.

Like the mafia, when you engage darkness of any kind, you have an entire team of embodied and disembodied beings who will support and enable you. The idea is to stand in your own light and enhance it, letting no one bend or influence you toward anything less than loving. This is terribly important especially in today's vitriolic society. The more evolved you become spiritually the more potent your energy and the more expeditious the karmic return of your actions.

An imprint lingers from all experiences and only needs your awakening or remembrance to trigger the memories. Keep in mind, you may not "remember" exact details, but you may have a feeling or a sense of it. Those who have been meditating for years might actually "see" their previous lives or relive them when going through spiritual processing.

Many people will tell you they have a sense that they were at Auschwitz or another death camp during Nazi rule. I can't tell you how many souls think they knew or were Mary Magdalene, and some may have actually been her disciples, post-Jesus' death. There have been some who had a fear of trains or planes, some fiercely afraid of drowning when there is no current-day rhyme or reason as to why. Children in particular are more aware of their past lives, but most parents dismiss their proclamations as imagination or fantasy. Children are naturally more awake by mere virtue of having been on the other side of the veil so recently. Parents, please pay particular attention to their drawings, ramblings, and behaviors, especially their fears. Notice their birthmarks too, for those are scarring from previous incarnations.

Birthmarks can reveal a great deal about previous lives and the depth of the emotional or physical trauma. In one case, I noticed imprints of puncture marks all over a client's body and legs. When I asked about it, she remarked that they were "weird," but she'd had them since birth. As we got deeper into the session, I saw a farm and it appeared to be the late 1800s or early 1900s. As I took her deep into regression, she fell into an almost trance-like state. Suddenly she clutched her legs and curled into a ball right in front of me, screaming, "Stop, please, stop!" The memory jolted her out of the altered state she was in and she began to wail.

Upon further investigation, she told me that she saw herself as a 14-year-old girl on a rural farm somewhere in the Midwest. Her parents left her alone for only a few hours when a neighborhood teenaged boy broke into her home and raped her. He then stabbed her to death with a ballpoint pen. She sobbed and shook with fear for only seconds, then, as is typically the case, the "seeing" of it initiated the process of healing. The altered state perception usually includes subtle information, which helps the seer understand "why" it happened. In other words, you may get a sense of karma or other lessons derived from such a horrific event. She continued and instantly it all made sense. She and her husband had repeatedly argued over where to live. He wanted to live out in the country on a ranch-style property, but her fear was so great that she refused, saying she would only live in the suburbs. It is not surprising that today, five years later, they live on the outskirts of town, on a three-acre ranch.

That familiarity you feel with a total stranger—or worse, the chill that runs up your spine when you meet a stranger who has harmed you in another incarnation—all have meaning and purpose, yet most people ignore it. Ailments, such as phantom pain for which there is no obvious reason or sudden aches that last only a few days then never return, are all imprints. There are imprints left over from difficult or stillborn births, cellular memories of rape, torture, deprivation, starvation, and the entire spectrum of human and physical emotion.

It is ironic that the more lovely moments of life seem to pass through us. On rare occasion, there are a few who recall the pleasantries of a lifetime. It is far more common that the cellular imprint is one of trauma, drama, or emotional upheaval because those are the events which set deeply into the heart and alter the biochemistry—which, in turn, stays the trauma.

Humankind has been on this Earth for approximately seven million years, and every soul, with rare exception, returns time and time again. Modern man has only evolved over the last four hundred years or so. The average person has had between 80-200 lives over the past 7 million years, depending on how quickly they moved up the tree of life. There are no new souls, thus imprints remain from many incarnations. All souls return to this amazing planet to improve life and the quality of their own and typically return to advance spiritually. Though not always the case, returning time and again offers a host of benefits for growth and learning, which eventually leads to serving others.

Chapter 8

Random Purpose

On February 4, 2015, I woke up in the middle of the night yelling to an Asian man named "Mr. Lin." In my dream, I urged him to grab hold of his wife and small child and hurry. "Move from the left side of the plane to the right side!" I screamed. *"Hurry!"* He responded quickly and did exactly as I told him, much to my surprise. My screaming at him woke me once I saw he had moved over.

I woke up with a feeling of peace mixed with anticipation and, as with many of these types of "dreams," I posted about it in social media at five in the morning. As is my morning routine, I turned on the television to see the horrific video of TransAsia flight 235, which had crashed into the Taipei Bridge in Taiwan, killing forty-three people. But fifteen passengers survived. I was speechless. A "friend" in social media read my post and messaged me about the BBC interviewing a few of the survivors, and one of them was the man I'd screamed at in my dreams: Mr. Lin. The following is that interview.

"Taiwanese couple Lin Mingwei and Jiang Yuying were traveling on the plane with their two-year-old son, Lin Riyao.

Local media said Lin Mingwei had changed seats from the left-hand side to the right before take-off because he was unsettled by a noise coming from the wing, something that might have saved their lives.

He was seated near where the fuselage broke apart, so when the plane was submerged, he was able to get out and help his wife to scramble out of the opening. They then found their son floating in the water, Taiwan's Central News Agency (CNA) reported. Lin Mingwei gave him CPR before rescuers arrived. ~BBC News

Nothing is random. There is a purpose for every moment of every lifetime, and we often fail to gauge the significance in events like the above mentioned. Could I have dismissed it as random or subconscious dreaming? Might I have ignored it and never followed up by watching the news? Yes, but I am constantly aware of the law of community which states that we take care of each other, whether stranger, friend, or foe. Did I personally know Mr. Lin? Not in this lifetime, but it is apparent I had to have known him in another place and time, or this event would not have occurred.

Why was he chosen for me to warn? I have no idea, and frankly it doesn't matter, but clearly there was and is purpose for him and his family to continue on Earth. When you understand the basic laws of humanity, you learn that ordinary people are purposeful every day, and many times are used to make a difference in ways which may seem unusual. I have learned to allow, rather than control, and as an instrument to remain open to serving others, wherever there is a need.

Lifetime after lifetime, we collect moments of grace like these and often credit angels, when in fact, it was another human spirit lending a hand. Angels are disembodied souls in etheric form, who remain in service to all living creation. Events like the TransAsia crash are a great catalyst to learn how to meditate and raise your frequency while evolving your spiritual gifts so you can be useful in multidimensional ways. There is nothing quite as rewarding as being in service to help souls you will never actually meet. Meditation is one of many ways to tap into your past lives, but asking the right questions and searching your soul for the answers is imperative. Meek and meager are fine, but bold and persistent is the way to awaken the deepest memories sleeping within you. Additionally, divine timing plays a critical role.

Years ago, right after my experience in the Alps, two women showed up at our home in Encino, California, announcing, "We know many of your previous incarnations." I am not one who relishes egos, so to have strangers recite the list of some roles I've played on Earth was daunting, to say the least. When one role in particular was mentioned, I found myself defensive and in denial. Resistance is a red flag, but evidently, it was not time to awaken that particular lifetime.

Six years later, it was.

We moved from Encino, California to Sedona, Arizona, then on to Colorado. By autumn, we were nestled into our three-story home in a well-established neighborhood. There had been little time to make new friends, so it was surprising when our neighbors called to invite us to dinner. In the middle of the call, one of our neighbors—Sue—asked if I was going to watch a two-part mini-series, the first half airing that night. To my surprise, I once again became defensive and told her I had no intention of watching it. But I did.

My husband was a few hours away on business, so I sat in my Lazy Boy chair and watched this epic tale with my arms crossed over my body, as if I were arguing with myself. The first night, I had little to no reaction; my guard was up too high to "feel" or "sense" anything. Two nights later, the second part aired, and to my surprise, I flew out of my chair onto my knees during one particular scene, compelled by energy far greater than me. I wailed out loud and screamed at the television in *fluent French* for ten minutes. Until that moment, I had never spoken French. I caught myself and snapped out of it, surely thinking the men with the little white coats were just around the corner. I began soothing myself with words like, *"I'm okay, it's not me!"* That did it. Denial and harboring, refusal to accept my own truth sealed my fate.

The next morning, I woke up with congestion and my throat was raw. I had not been sick with even a cold since that wondrous death in the Alps so long ago, so I was stymied with confusion. My husband called from the road and, hearing my voice, asked, "What in the world is going on?" I told him what had happened, to which he wisely replied, "Meditate on it."

Later that evening, we got a call from Germany. My mother-in-law, in a non-emotional voice, told us that my father-in-law had suffered a stroke. We had just returned a month earlier from our annual trip to his small village in Southwest Germany, so we were in no financial position to return so soon. From our home, I did what I could with my healing gifts while still trying to wrap my brain around my own spiritual freak show.

By Saturday morning, I was in full-blown denial, with a severe case of laryngitis from "swallowing" my truth. I was in so much denial, wanting nothing to do with this particular lifetime, that I had also formed a rash around both of my swollen eyes, which took the form of a pair of eyeglasses. I was refusing to "see" my truth as well. I became so frustrated that in a strained whisper, I screamed out, *"Okay! Okay! Maybe I had something to do with that lifetime!"* Within 20 minutes of owning my truth, even if hesitantly, my voice returned, the rash was gone, and I was back to normal. Well, normal, if you consider anything about this "normal."

The next morning while sitting in church, my husband whispered, "My father is asking for us to come. He's not improving. Why don't you check on airline tickets and see how much they are?"

It was mid-June with summer travel in high gear. I phoned the airlines and, of course, there were no tickets available to

Frankfurt, Germany due to high travel season. I pleaded and informed the ticket agent of my father-in-law's stroke and our need to get there quickly. I asked, "Did you try flights to Munich?"

"None," she replied.

I said, "Okay, would you please try flights to Stuttgart, Salzburg, and Dusseldorf?"

After a long wait, she returned. "Sorry, there are no seats available on any of those flights."

"Please, try London, Gatwick, and Heathrow!"

"Ma'am, there are no flights to Germany from England. All booked."

My chest sank but as is always the case, a divine hand intercepted. "Wait," she paused. "Didn't you tell me that you had some mileage points?"

I scrambled to look for the exact number in my husband's mileage plus account. *Yes! We have one hundred and nine thousand miles! But what difference does it make if there are no flights?*

In a rather excited voice she spoke, "For one hundred thousand miles, I can fly you into Paris for only $29.95 each."

"What?!" Had I heard her correctly? "How is that possible?"

"You only have to pay the taxes, and you can leave first thing in the morning. Once you arrive in Paris, you can drive to Germany or pick up an inner Europe flight to Frankfurt."

Suddenly, it hit me: France would awaken, validate, solidify, and hopefully heal the trauma and regrets leftover from hundreds of years—and all for the bargain price of $29.95. We departed the next day, arriving in Paris early the following morning. It had only been one week since the onslaught of memories had unsuspectedly been triggered by a television mini-series. We drove to Germany and, once there, made a mad dash to the hospital to see my father-in-law.

Aware of the heat and energy that comes from my hands, my father-in-law Rudi immediately "assumed the position," bragging to his roommate aloud, *"Das ist meine schwiggertochter, sie ist eine heiler"* (This is my daughter-in-law; she is a healer!). Rudi was a funny little man who didn't believe in much, having been ripped from his home by Nazis at age six and thrown into the Hitler youth camps. He was scarred by racism and scorned by his peers for something he had no control over. Thus, he went through his life with as little gusto as is humanly possible, a house painter with little motivation and without any desire to be more. He was essentially a child emotionally and with every ailment became more so, a burden my mother-in-law relished and enabled, even cutting his meat for him. But I loved him and was eager to see him out of pain and danger, so I did what the Holy Spirit guided me to do. Within an hour, he was about 80 percent better and ready to go home. He left the hospital the very next day and returned home to the comfort of his own bed. My mother-in-law assumed it was the medication that sped up his recovery, much to the amusement of my husband and me.

We left the following day, driving back to Paris—a seven-hour drive at the time. We planned to spend the very next day exploring the area which held the trauma I experienced centuries ago. The next morning, we woke early and there was palatable fear in my spirit and my body ached. I knew the day would be one I would never forget. We drove for what seemed like endless hours to the exact location where time and history collided with the present day. The sky was pouring down rain, which seemed befitting, given it was almost like a baptismal cleansing, washing away the pangs of the past. My husband parked the car and, as if I were no longer in control of my body, I leapt from the car before he had come to a full stop.

My heart was racing with fear, and the remembrance of years long gone was now in the present. I didn't need to search a map or even ask a stranger where to go; my feet walked a rampant steady pace as I wandered back in time down streets of cobblestone. I was transfixed with how similar it all looked, even though hundreds of years had passed. I retraced the steps held in my consciousness, my heart beating faster with every familiar marker I passed, and to my amazement, many still stood hundreds of years later.

Suddenly, it was before me. My eyes rested upon the epicenter of those historical events. Like a treasure chest of heartache and betrayal, I sat on the ancient wall which surrounded a place seared into my memory because of what took place there. Time had altered very little; the wall still imprisoned the horrors of that time, now etched in stone. I sat, tears streaming down my face, a conversation with God falling from my lips, stammering and vague. The heavens, to no surprise, answered back, with distinct clarity. Each word humbled me to stillness, silence, and introspection. I was absorbing information at the speed of light, unaware of the meandering tourists trotting past me. Even loud and often obnoxious Americans could not interrupt this reprise.

My husband wandered through the shops which lined the area, knowing and honoring that I would be in a holy conference, battling for the restitution of my soul. My tears dried as the breeze kissed my face, and I was ready to move on to the next pinnacle location, one where more cruelty took place. This one was more difficult to locate, probably because I was unprepared for what came next.

After walking in the scorching sun for what seemed like forever, we rounded a corner and, like a scar embedded in the foreboding clouds, there it was; the stone cage where unspeakable atrocities took place. Without warning, I began to hurl. There I was in a charming French village shamelessly spewing onto the ancient cobblestone streets. My husband looked horrified as I waved him to go on and leave me there in my awkward humiliation. This was not a moment that I wanted any attention or to be fawned over. The moment invaded my soul, hundreds of years of torment, self-loathing, and fear longing to be released, the trepidation of my own ghost incarnate.

My husband returned swiftly. "The site is closed; this is the only day of the week it isn't open."

Why was I not surprised? In any lifetime, you will never be given more than you can bear, and I had reached my limit after such a long day. We drove back in silence as the city lights faded into rolling hills and shadows. I was certain I would never have to revisit that lifetime again. I was certain that I'd seen and felt enough to last me a thousand more lifetimes. I was eager to forget and ignore the mushroom cloud welling up inside me. Surely, I had done enough to exhaust, integrate, and forgive myself and those who had harmed me. I was wrong.

It took three trips in three years to return to the shadows of such a potent and painful life. With each trip, I began to acclimate and evolve, and perspective was born from taking personal responsibility. At the end of our last trip, I can honestly say my soul was lighter and more at peace. I integrated the strengths from that lifetime and discarded the pain. I forgave myself for choosing all of it, now understanding the probable karma which caused the effect. The last piece of the puzzle came when I returned home from our very last trip.

Before bed, I prayed and consulted with my angels and guides, seeking to be shown what I had done to set up the dynamics of that lifetime. Remember, directly or indirectly, we choose it all. As always, my dream was vivid and lacked any ambiguity. I was shown a lifetime I'd lived two hundred years earlier. I was a ruler in a nearby region, a good man, but one who was a wee bit overzealous and complex. It was abundantly clear I had pursued and persecuted an entire religious sect of people, who had in turn returned in mass to repay that negative karma, tenfold. When I woke from this enlightening epiphany, these words fell from my lips: "Well, (sigh) I deserved it then."

Instantly upon taking personal responsibility, my soul was free. Forgiveness is essential to personal well-being but only comes when you acknowledge your missteps. It wasn't those who hurt me I had to forgive; I had to forgive myself for what I did to harm others beforehand and had to forgive myself for choosing such a difficult role. By action, word, or deed, we choose it all, and I had gotten what I had given, two hundred years earlier.

After researching both characters, I found the similarities and segues incredible. The lives of these two characters paralleled, even living in some of the same regions and shot by an arrow in the same exact location of their bodies, two hundred years apart. Again, this was a classic example of cellular memory. Additionally, their travels paralleled to some of the same regions in two countries. I thoroughly exhausted all the intersections of two people, two lifetimes which held the secrets to so much about the workings within this present-day woman. After extensive research and reconciliation, I made peace with these aspects of my soul.

It was over. Now the dead could truly rest in peace and I could move on, stronger, more awake, more aware, and ever so grateful. The gift was awareness; yes, I had suffered but by my own hand. I created the karma. I did that to me—no one else, just me. Those who participated in that lifetime had generated their own karma, and I am sure that over time they've repaid theirs as well. Don't worry what others do, for they, like you, will get in return what they give. Focus on your own past and present-life karma and how to heal it.

The lessons garnered from exploring these two lifetimes were enormous. I felt only gratitude to have listened to the sounds of my clanging soul, longing to be freed from the chains that held me captive to a past which no longer served me. An interesting note: I had been to France many times before this and loathed it, the rudeness of the French people in particular. Once I integrated and healed that lifetime, stripping away the shadows and veils, I freed my love for all things French again, even the people.

Powerful events are seared into the soul. I liken the remembrance of intention, emotional fervor, and physical torment to a box of boomerangs. What's surprising is that even the subtle experiences, like being lied to or betrayed, often sleep in the memory. They wake only when the memory is triggered, typically by the reoccurrence of a similar scenario. How nice it would be if karma was written visibly on the body so humans didn't continue to repeat behaviors which create more negative karma.

I am alarmed by those who create negatively then wonder why their lives become undone. There is an outcome for every thought. The universe is not punishing you; it's responding to you. Everything you think becomes audible energy and your thoughts are received throughout the universe, gathering the same or like energy along the path of sojourn. When you become aware of just how potent your words are, you learn to employ the alchemy of the sages and masters who have graced this Earth with ancient wisdom and eloquent teachings. You soon learn to amplify your messages more deliberately, recognizing that every thought generates a response in the universe.

Memories are seared and scored by your experiences and perceptions. You don't necessarily need to know who you've been, what you've done, or how much you've gone through. However, when memories begin to surface (as they do in all souls, though most dismiss or run to the doctor), it is incumbent on you to, at the very least, pray and meditate on what is trying to surface. Pain is not random; it is your body trying to talk to you, attempting to wake up your mind and spirit. The soul seeks absolution; it longs to be reunited with its broken pieces to unveil its purest essence.

In the "seeing" or "knowing" of such impactive moments in time, healing is often waiting at the end—not just physically, but emotionally too. It may take a week, a year, or many years to process your dreams, memories, or physical anomalies, but addressing them head on is the way to integrate and evolve. To heal the mind, body, and soul and relieve it of sorrow, loss, abandonment, jealousy, envy, greed, addiction, rage, or fear is a noble goal. Tenacity, persistence, timing, and a willingness to engage the unconscious is elementary to uncovering memories. You must be willing to accept that you are not the same person you were in decades past. You mustn't feel guilty for whatever you may have done in another lifetime. There's no need for soul bashing, and it serves no purpose.

The universe does not punish anyone; that concept is religious rhetoric which stokes fear in unwitting souls. There is no God above you that will make you take responsibility for your actions in any lifetime. It simply doesn't work that way. Having died and learned more on the other side than in entire lifetimes freed me of that dogmatic notion. Many times, your dreams will try to show you previous lifetimes, but only the most astute student of spirituality will take dreams seriously and learn how to decipher and access the answers you are seeking. Dreams are the universal way of connecting, and often it is more than just the subconscious at work.

The actress and comedian extraordinaire Melissa McCarthy was on the *Ellen DeGeneres* show during the COVID-19 pandemic alongside her husband Ben Falcone. She was telling Ellen about a dream she had. In the dream, she and her family were quarantined inside their home, but to her surprise, Mark Wahlberg was living in their guestroom. Melissa went on to say it was a six-hour dream and that he was a great roommate, even admitting that when she woke, she went downstairs to make sure he wasn't actually in the guest room. Most people, including Ellen, would automatically think that maybe Melissa watched a Wahlberg movie which remained in her subconscious. Dreams can be a byproduct of the subconscious; however, those who understand reincarnation, past lives, or have a strong connection to God, their guides, and angels recognize it is often so much more.

Dreams are the internal messengers of the soul, the cellular megaphone that often is speaking to the person who is dreaming. In Melissa's case, Mark Wahlberg is a part of her soul group, meaning they have been together in many previous incarnations. Whether they were siblings, parent/child, neighbors, enemies, or romantically entangled is something they alone would have to explore. It is rare to dream about someone randomly if you've never known them, unless you are dreaming about someone who is yet to come into your life.

I've had dreams with specific names given, and after intensive research could not figure out why. That is when I make a conscious decision to simply pray for that person. You don't have to know a person to direct angels to assist them through prayer. Sometimes, the very names I've dreamt are of people who I meet later down the road and immediately recall the dream. It not only enhances the relationship, but dreams may offer advanced insight into more about that person or scenario.

Years ago, I had a visceral dream about Tony Robbins, the author, speaker, and life coach who has sold countless books and inspired many. To be completely transparent, I was neither a fan nor follower, nor was I connected to him via social media, so there was no reason for me to have a dream about him other than a divine appointment. In the dream, it was morning and I logged into Twitter to see Tony Robbins trending. I dreamed he'd died unexpectedly and all of Twitter was lit with his fans in full-blown mourning. I woke up suddenly and tears had fallen onto my pillow. It was real, visceral, and deeply upsetting despite the fact that I was simply not a fan.

I scrambled urging the universe to tell me what to do, knowing that when things like this are shown to me, there is time to redirect the scenario. The universe often functions on the principle of: "to be forewarned is to be forearmed."

I immediately logged into Twitter to make sure it hadn't already happened, that he was in fact, still alive. Then, I sent a tweet to Tony. I could not tell him what I dreamed because there is always a risk that you will set the actions into motion if the object of your dream begins to fear or obsess over it. Instead, I tweeted something to the effect that it was urgent I speak with him. He immediately followed me on Twitter then sent me a direct message, "What's going on?"

In a roundabout way, I mentioned I'd had a dream about him, and without telling him the details I simply urged him to be cautious for the next thirty to sixty days. Tony is very athletic and at the time was known for participating in extreme sports. We bantered back and forth; it was a dance that had me on my toes, balancing the information with a firm warning. He thanked me, and then, to my surprise, concluded our conversation with telling me he loved my voice and had downloaded two songs I'd recorded to his iPod. Who would have thunk it? Needless to say, prayers and forewarning shifted his circumstances, and he continues to live and thrive happily today in 2021.

Nothing is random, and everything is purposeful.

Chapter 9

Real or Surreal?

Let's talk about the elephant in the room: how do you know if you are imagining a past life event or if it's real? Only a small percent of human beings attempt to decipher their dreams or visions. For those on a spiritual path, past life exploration is a natural segue to spiritual healing and evolution. It is more common in children to have predominant past life memories surface, and thankfully, there are plenty of medical doctors, researchers, and psychiatrists worldwide who specialize in navigating these extraordinary cases. In adults, it is often very subtle and can be triggered by current circumstances, events, or through meditation or other spiritual practices. There are other validating factors unique to the person having the memories. Hypnosis, breathwork, and past life regression are not easily fooled when facilitated by qualified practitioners, especially those who specialize in this field.

As mentioned earlier, those stronger personalities with distinct characteristics often return to Earth looking very similar to what they looked like in a previous incarnation. Often, the strongest memories are those lived within the last 500 years.

With reams of records and data passed down throughout history, there is usually a trail of information to uncover with a simple google search.

Many of the six million Jewish lives that were taken in the Holocaust returned within twenty or thirty years of those events, since their lives were prematurely snuffed out. Some came back as Germans, so they could try to understand how an entire nation could be so blind to fascism and allow such horrors to occur. Some returned as leaders to ensure that history never repeats itself, and some returned as healers, nurturers, officials, politicians, artists, photographers, and others simply as good parents. There is always a rebirth of souls who collectively pass away, those who produce massive change, especially after major disasters or tragedies.

The victims of the RMS Titanic and the RMS Lusitania are another example where there are reams of validating information, images, and film footage of those who sailed aboard these vessels. Many of those souls returned rather quickly as well. Where there is premature death, the soul group will often return within 100 years or less. Look closely at director James Cameron, writer and Academy Award-winning director of the movie, *Titanic*. The resemblance to the captain of the *Titanic*, Captain Edward John Smith, is nothing short of remarkable. Smith was so perplexed by the sinking of what was lauded as being "the unsinkable Titanic," that he returned to Earth only forty-two years later to investigate the disaster and create an amazing account of its sinking so history would finally know what happened. It was his way to ensure that there was accountability—to heal the karma he incurred by being complicit and to set the record straight. If you study some of the other characters sailing on that vessel, you will find many of them returned to Earth and worked with Cameron on the movie. Imagine having the ability to relive your previous life on a massive movie set with the ability to see today what you could not see in that previous lifetime.

Naturally, there are so many lifetimes where names cannot be recovered or there is no history to record. Those are people who simply lived obscure lives and whom no one really knows existed. In those cases, names are not essential, though can still be surfaced through various modalities such as hypnosis and regression. All roles are important and fulfill some purpose. Often, those whose names did not make the history books are the very people that made some of the greatest contributions to life. We know few names of those who built the pyramids, Manchu Pichu, and Chichen Itza. In a world this vast, there have been so many contributions made by nameless, faceless ancients.

Do all souls who return have similar defects, fears, talents, physical similarities, and so on? Not necessarily. But if they return quickly within twenty years or less, the imprint will be stronger. In 1994, Oprah Winfrey had a little, red-haired, snow-white-skinned boy on her show. His name is Chase Bowman. In 1988, five-year-old Chase suddenly became terrified by fireworks. It was the Fourth of July holiday, and he was terrified by the popping noises coming from outside. His mother, Carol, thought it odd since it had never happened before. His fear grew, so Carol turned to a friend who was a hypnotherapist. During their session, Chase recalled a battlefield during the Civil War. He could see himself behind a rock, holding a big gun. He also saw a black soldier being shot. "Chase" was shot in the wrist and sent to a field hospital. After being bandaged, he was sent back to the front line where it was his job to fire a cannon. He remembered being killed during the battle. Chase was able to draw the battlefield, including specific details—the hospital and the precise location of his own gunshot wound. Civil war historians were able to validate his accurate drawings.

Today, Chase Bowman is a cinematographer and actor enjoying a successful career. Carol went on to become an author, lecturer, counselor, and therapist known for her work in studying cases of reincarnation, especially those involving young children. Chase is one of millions who go from being black to Caucasian and vice versa. From one race to another, one belief to the opposite, we are ever evolving as souls.

You've heard stories of heart transplant patients receiving a new organ then suddenly having a craving for beer, or they are suddenly sentimental when they weren't prior to the transplant. Cellular memories remain in the organs, imprinted from multitudes of previous lifetime experiences.

"How do human genetics factor in?" In his book *Ageless Mind, Timeless Body*, author, speaker, and medical doctor Deepak Chopra spoke of cellular regeneration and how the average human body regenerates enough new cells in each organ that you basically get a new body every year. In other words, the body is constantly repairing itself, and what you eat, how you treat your body, and what you feed your mind all factor into the total sum of wellness. Age will still eventually diminish the human body; however, the fountain of youth truly lies within perception, nutrition, and a host of other variables, including your consciousness and healing cellular memories.

Science has proven that even genes can be transmuted, and humans are not slaves to genetic family history. In essence, your body has the ability to heal itself, and even genetics can be transmuted. Cellular memory stems from the soul, so no matter what body you incarnate into, the imprints enter at the time of birth and remain until you address them. The most impactful memories awaken more with your own spiritual awakening. One has nothing to do with the other. Genetics, epigenetics are physical traits, cellular memory is consciousness-based and is only transferred into the physical body at the time of birth.

Though we have far to go in understanding the mysteries of the human body, mind, and spirit connection, it is abundantly clear that you have more power over your personal health and over aging than you imagine. Thoughts are the catalyst for well-being, but reactions are the hypocenter. How you respond, react, and digest interactions with others determines the outcome in most cases. Emotional response will either empower you or undo you. Your thoughts on every topic that concerns you will seed and feed the way your body processes the information. While the body is capable of healing itself, your thoughts must be aligned to a positive or optimistic flow of energy in order to begin the regenerative process.

When returning to Earth, how do you choose? It begins with what you seek to accomplish while on the Earth. Souls consult with sages—those wise souls many humans call "angels" or "masters"—and collectively review Akashic records (the database of everything that you've said, thought, or done) also known Biblically as "The Lamb's Book of Life." Why would anyone choose a life of abuse or addiction? Why would you choose a life where you are murdered or imprisoned? It doesn't work like that. No one chooses to be killed or addicted, diseased, or mentally ill. Karma, the law of cause and effect, factors into your choice. Race, logistics, career choices, and a multitude of varying dynamics with others in your soul group are also taken into consideration. There are a host of other variables applied to those who are handicapped or have special needs.

There are certain preferences and characteristics we choose upon return. For example, if you have always favored long hair, you will most likely choose to have long hair in subsequent lifetimes; if you prefer blonde over brunette, or short and petite versus tall and medium build, it is probable you will continue choosing a similar frame and size. Most souls decide approximately how long to stay on Earth in order to accomplish the majority of everything they have considered.

Many people tell me they are afraid they will come back as an animal, but I must emphasize, the soul only evolves forward, never backward. In the beginning, souls inhabited the Earth in primitive forms but once you have been human, you do not digress. It would be impossible to be a rationalizing, intelligent human being and then suddenly return as an animal. You would go mad; the senses are too strong for a human to embody an animal. However, animals often become quite human in their behavior and mimic their owner's behavior, such as smiling, frowning, opening doors, and in some cases, speaking like a human.

Why do some souls return to a new life with the ability to play the piano or score great musical compositions and others don't? It depends on the levels of passion you hold in your consciousness. Intention, passion, and events which impacted or impressed you linger in the memory banks of consciousness. If you've ever had a favorite musical or visual artist, or if you've dreamed of singing or playing an instrument and aren't able to in the present lifetime, chances are you will return with those particular skills at some point in the future.

Another contributing factor is the level of mastery you have accomplished. If you have chosen well, you will have run the gambit on lifetimes and awakened and evolved your consciousness. It is one of the many reasons some have a conscious glimpse of their past and why some can tap into those lifetimes. The more awake, aware, and unblemished your consciousness is, the greater the view. Shadows cast shadows and create barriers to the higher light, or your ability to access the pure god-self or superconscious. It is one of the most reveling feelings in the world to be able to access those elements of your existence which dim or even diminish your access to the superconscious mind. That supreme paradigm, the superconscious, is what many call the God realm. The superconscious is primarily a level of awareness that goes beyond material reality. Many in the spiritual community call it the "ether," or the essence of the universe. It is a flow of electromagnetic waves that permeate all matter and space, where all wisdom is not only accessible but divine.

It is the definitive realm where all answers dwell.

Chapter 10

Goodness is Gold

Every soul perceives its personal experiences differently. Some will fold under the smallest slight, while others rise to a new level of success. Some use pain as a catalyst to become more, to succeed more, and to understand others better. Others see pain as the ultimate saboteur of their happiness and fall headfirst into the role of victim.

Pain is useless without its counterpart, pleasure, as one without the other eliminates the need to heal. There are none who escape life pain-free, none. Pain, whether physical, emotional, or both, stimulate certain degrees of consciousness and delineate characteristics essential to the development of character. Some of these characteristics or attributes include:

- Resilience
- Courage
- Integrity
- Forthrightness
- Tenacity
- Honesty

- Compassion
- Loyalty
- Dependability
- Discipline
- Self-love
- Confidence
- Faith
- Endurance
- Optimism
- Self-reliance
- Self-soothing
- Discernment
- Forgiveness
- Kindness
- Wisdom

Tell a child that the stove is hot, and he will typically touch it anyway and get burned. It is how he learns discernment, and often how to take instruction. A young lady's boyfriend cheats on her, which may enforce or teach forgiveness, discernment, and honesty, or may make her bitter and trigger commitment or abandonment issues. A politician has a huge fall from grace and may learn tenacity, courage, forthrightness, and resilience, or he might become agoraphobic. The depth of a person's individual consciousness determines how many times a human must repeat lessons in order to evolve.

Consciousness is a creature of choice, an amalgam of infinite choices, experiences, and a culmination of everything you've been, done, and learned. Consciousness is the purest form of awareness. Every memory, even those your mind has blocked or forgotten, remains as an imprint. That imprint follows you into every existence until you have addressed and dealt with the damage and shadows left behind. Once you've exhausted the shadows and purged limiting imprints, they are transmuted.

The caveat is that you are a constant, ever-changing collection of atoms and energy. All matter is made up of atoms and molecules which act like an ecosystem. As you change your thoughts, perception, and reactions, you alter the quality of your cellular composition and life follows suit. With heightened consciousness and by maintaining a higher frequency, you can transverse cellular biology as well as the genome composition.

Love is the core component of the soul, while goodness originates from the purity of your spirit. A few years ago, I had a consult with a modern-day royal who was struggling emotionally, and in the midst of the conversation, he blurted out, "Ariaa, you always do the right thing!" I attribute that core impulse or characteristic to many lifetimes of learning what the right thing is. However, many don't know that as you evolve, you develop a conscience and a kind of barometer which gauges goodness and the right use of will. This doesn't mean you're a bad person if you don't know what the right thing is. As you deepen your awareness, you grow intellectually and spiritually, and the "right thing" becomes evident for most humans.

For the very first time, a friend discovered the sheer bliss of doing the right thing. Vince was working in a big city and decided to enjoy some Indian food for lunch. With the rushed lunch crowd, it was just the sort of place where no one was really paying attention to anyone else. It was "sit wherever you'd like" seating, and as Vince approached a booth, there was what appeared to be a woman's pocketbook sitting on the seat.

Normally, Vince would think, "lucky me" and might have taken the attitude of, "not my circus, not my monkeys!" However, something profound happened; he thought of this stranger and how panicked she must be, as there was a lot of cash hanging out of the edges and her credit cards and driver's license were stuffed inside. He suddenly, compassionately walked in her shoes.

He reacted swiftly, never counting the money or having any thought other than, "I have to get this back to the woman who left it here." He managed to find the woman's phone number and called. She let out a sigh of relief, telling Vince how panicked she was and asking him to leave it with the restaurant manager. Knowing he would be late to work, he chose to go the extra mile and stayed for another hour waiting for her to return, concerned that someone else might not do the right thing. It was a proud moment for a man who was accustomed to his first thought, in a scenario like this, being anything but noble. It was such a gratifying moment, Vince experienced that "givers high," and it permanently altered the way he thinks for the better.

Dishonesty and misaligned intentions result in misery, feelings of guilt, and the return of negative karma. Human consciousness often develops by learning what not to do.

Forming a fully developed consciousness and the highest path of greater understanding is paramount to the continuity of the species. Exploring opposite polarities is a natural part of evolution; in fact, the universe is built on opposite polarities.

You wouldn't know what love is if you've never experienced hate.

You wouldn't know what forgiveness is if you'd never been forgiven.

You would not know what humility is if you've never been humiliated or had your own arrogance backfire on you.

You wouldn't know what rich is if you've never been poor.

You wouldn't know what joy is if not for sadness.

You wouldn't recognize contentment if you've never been discontent.

You would not know peace without chaos or war.

You would not know security without fear.

You wouldn't feel confident unless you've been insecure at some point in time.

You wouldn't know self-love without self-loathing.

You would not know what sacrifice is if you have never had to give up anything.

You would not know what charity is if you've never been in need.

You wouldn't know what justice is if you've never been accused, falsely or otherwise.

Kindness and goodness are symbiotic and run akin to a seed, both a half of the whole. You cannot be kind without being good, and you cannot be good without being kind. In a world where the darkness is amplified, goodness is the balm that helps sustain the light in the world. Every heroic or selfless act adds density to the light. Every kind word or deed fills pockets of void, where nothingness is transformed into tangible fields of love. Love is the consummate umbrella which deflects the all-consuming mist of hate and shields you from the flood of ignorance. Good works continue to live long after you're gone, and if you are wise, you return to carry on the works you began in previous incarnations. Not everyone will return to the same or a similar path, but those who do usually accomplish more than those who don't.

A servant's heart is a heart full of love and doesn't stop at helping others. In fact, helping others is intuitive and instinctive, and the purest intention is the one which never gives a second thought to the cost. While all humans have a particular calling or platform in life, a mastered soul serves the Earth, the creatures, and the humans. It is the single most important lesson that living on Earth offers; that we are all here to love and serve one another.

"If humans realized they return time and time again, they would treat others with more kindness and would treat the Earth with greater respect."

Chapter 11

The Gateway

I love elderly folks—always have. I've volunteered at assisted living centers for more than twenty-eight years because the wisdom and history seniors have experienced is always a source of fascination for me. Those in their eighties and nineties are filled with sensational tales of war and automobiles, airplanes, and ships that set sail across the oceans, to take them to places they only dreamed of seeing.

The elderly are always quick to share a story of how they had to walk to school or work, and usually in "brutal" conditions while traversing "gargantuan" distances (two to ten miles is the average length based on the hundreds of conversations I've had with these souls). Then sadness mixed with fear will suddenly set into the lines of their ancient faces as they begin to speak of death or recognize how little time is left. Often, they sit staring out the window, as if they can capture time in a bottle and slow down the inevitable.

When you ask, many will tell you that they don't fear death, but almost all will tell you they are more concerned about how they will die. It is suffering they fear most. Dying is as natural as being born, but you don't remember your own birth. Consciousness and the awareness of death play an enormous role in how and when you are going to die. For the awakened soul, it has little to do with genetics or even sickness.

Years ago, I had a neighbor whose father moved in with her after the passing of his wife of fifty-four years. One day she mentioned that her dad wasn't doing well. "Is he sick?" I asked.

"No, but he is having temper fits and is taking his anger out on his body by not eating."

I asked Sue if I could go down to the basement where he was living and see what I could do to help, to which she eagerly replied, "Please!"

Walking down the stairs was like descending into a dungeon; don't get me wrong, they had a lovely home, but Al's energy was dark, angry, and palatable, and it filled every corner of the basement. I spoke in my usual bright-eyed, bushy-tailed, happy-go-lucky way, hoping it would shift his mood or, at the very least, garner a reaction from this depressed and angry man. "Hey, Al, how are you? You're looking mighty dapper!"

To my surprise, he was amiable and unguarded and began pouring out how frustrated he was, living in the basement when only two years earlier, he was living with his beloved wife in their beautiful home. We engaged in a comprehensive conversation about death and dying. He lamented that ever since his wife had died, he had been trying to leave Earth to be with her, to no avail. He was tired and angry at God and beleaguered, blaming the Lord for keeping him on the Earth in what he called a "hellhole."

I understood his frustration but assured him there was a way to "get out," not suggesting Dr. Kevorkian stop by for a visit. I told him to stop fighting, stop blaming, and most of all to get busy living and forget about dying for now. I suggested that at bedtime, he recite these simple words: "I surrender my will to live," "Into your hands I surrender my spirit," and again, I emphasized he say, "I surrender my will to God."

Two weeks later, I got the call. He didn't even realize how powerful he was, but alas, Al passed away at nine in the evening and his daughter was eagerly waiting for the coroner to arrive. I waited patiently outside in the cold, icy air of January so I could bid farewell to this lovely old soul.

After some time, the ambulance arrived, and the stretcher was rolled out to the curb. I asked the coroner if he would give me a moment to say goodbye and to give Al a kiss on the forehead. As the attendant lowered the sheet, you could hear me gasp all the way down the street through the crisp night air. I was startled beyond belief and quickly said, "Did you do that?"

"No—no, ma'am, I didn't!"

I said, "Did his daughter do that?"

He shook his head and said, "No, she told us that she didn't even touch the body. He died like that."

I was gobsmacked. Al looked like The Joker in Batman, his face relaxed but with the most animated, gigantic smile, I've ever seen, curled perfectly upward. It was abundantly evident that he did not suffer and was delighted to finally be out of his pain-filled body and reunited with his beloved wife. The joy was permanently seared into his face for all eternity.

Death should not be feared or dreaded when your time has come. It is simply a change of form from an Earth body, subject to limitations, to energy with ever-changing form. Dying is as natural as combing your hair. What you think, what you believe, and the choices you make determine the condition you're in at the time of your death. I'm always surprised at how many people try to run from death when their diagnosis is terminal. Spending hundreds of thousands of dollars to prolong life for a few months doesn't make sense to me, especially when you consider how sick chemo and radiation make a patient. What is the point of living a few months longer when you are bedridden from the treatment? I've always thought there is a better way to wrap up your life on Earth, and it isn't being poked, prodded, hospitalized, and fried by cancer treatments.

Though I haven't been sick with even a cold in more than a quarter of a century, I know what I would do if given a death sentence. Since I already have my obituary written, service planned, and all my possessions designated to friends and charities, I would be able to spend what little time is left in thoughtful ways. I would make video messages for all those I love to be played on their birthdays, anniversaries, birth of a child, or some other random occasion. Then I would travel, oh, how I do love traveling. All the countries deemed too dangerous to visit, I would put at the top of my list—after all, what would I have to lose? After visiting all the places on my list, I would return home and have all my friends and loved ones come by my house to take whatever they want while I was still alive.

I have been burdened over the years with having to clean out the houses of people I loved after they've died and find it an appalling process. It is an ardent task, for those who die in their seventies, eighties, or even nineties had years to dispense and rid themselves of all the clutter. Those charged with this task are often confused and mourning and rarely know what to do with someone else's treasures. I can't emphasize enough to get your affairs in order, especially after the Coronavirus pandemic, as you never know when you will leave the Earth. It is also prudent to plan your own funeral, cremation, or celebration of life ceremony, because when people are mourning, it is very challenging to put one together.

Pets left behind hit my heart the hardest. I can't imagine why an eighty-year-old person would get a puppy or kitten instead of an older pet, knowing they may not live long enough to take care of it. It is hard on a pet when their owner dies, and they are often sent packing to a stranger's home or a shelter, without anyone considering how the pet is feeling or if they will adjust. As of the current penning of this book, I will be sixty-five years of age soon and I know the four dogs I have now will not outlive me. I have two Chihuahuas who are ten years old and two Cockashons turning four this year. After these are gone, I will simply have to visit the shelters to pet strays and lost dogs and cats or adopt an elderly pet. Again, most of us know about how long we will live, it is innate—but I digress.

Many who have had near-death experiences have shared tales of such beautiful, paradisiacal realms and the peace felt instantly upon dying. My own death experience in the Alps during the early 90s was beyond descriptive and has left an indelible memory. Once you examine and embrace how vital reincarnation is, you begin to see its essential role in human dynamics. You begin to understand how important your choices are, the beliefs you subscribe to, and how every choice reaps blessings or karma. Instantly, suffering, handicaps, the mentally ill, deformation, trials, sexual identity, success, fears, and disease all make far more sense when viewed through the lens of consecutive lifetimes. You discover there are no victims, only souls who are unable to embrace that all choices have a ripple effect. Death is liberation and an opportunity to readjust your sails and chart a new course, navigating new worlds.

With each lifetime you gain, you lose, reap, sow, and harvest, rising up the scale of wisdom and knowledge to ultimately be transformed backward into your core composition. Once the veils are lifted, the purest essence of love is uncovered, and judgment ceases to exist. As humans, it is all forgotten when we return to Earth, save a rare few who are able to hold on to their highest self upon return.

With each life and death, you amass a greater density of light. Human frailties or that which mankind thinks of as mistakes are the multi-pathways which lead to greater understanding. Each lifetime leaves a series of imprints or anomalies, which if allowed to remain unaddressed, carry over into subsequent lifetimes.

A viable scenario would be someone who dies of brain cancer, then returns to Earth too soon, having not taken enough time on the other side to understand the probable cause in order to heal the anomaly. Thus, the new baby is born with a deformed brain or develops a brain tumor or injury in early life. This is how imprints work. They re-infect the body with the trauma of previous lifetimes unless you take the time while on Earth or in the heavens to understand, heal, and restore those emotions which negatively impacted the body. Your physical body may carry the imprint, but your emotional body houses the associated lower emotions like fear and suffering.

If you overcome the urge to succumb to those nuances or behaviors of old imprints, you heal and integrate the strengths from each incarnation while discarding the shadows and derogatory emotions. As you do, you strengthen who you are today and essentially become more complete and more whole as a functioning human being. If you are weak-willed today but the memory of a strong leader emerges, you will likely become a stronger leader today as you integrate and incorporate the ancient personality. If you have a fear of losing children because you did in a previous incarnation, you will overcome that fear with every passing year your present-day children grow. Hopefully sooner, if you choose to be self-aware and directly address the fear. Healing, integrating, discarding, and completing the unfinished cycles of life are some of the many benefits of past life memories.

Chapter 12

The Evolution of Animals

Your pets come back to you! Like people, animals return time and time again too, and many of your pets are the reincarnation of one of your previous or past life's pets. They can also be animals who you have encountered in olden times, such as sheep, wolves, or livestock who enjoyed your energy enough to return as your domesticated pet.

Animals evolve up the chain of life and achieve in their world, just as humans do in theirs. They also have their own karma and evolve by working through their own life lessons. They too evolve their consciousness and, at some point of evolution, inhabit a human body. The soul never goes backward, always forward, always higher in consciousness, even if a soul remains the same in development over several lifetimes. One never goes from human to animal; it would simply be too hard to erase a human level of existence to do so, not to mention how cumbersome that would be.

Animals, just like humans, reincarnate as they continue up the scale of evolution and growth. Life evolves in every species and animals move from one form to another, repaying karma and learning just as humans do—so what happened in 1999 was of no surprise to me. I had a little short-haired Chihuahua named Kibbles who was the absolute love of my life. On a winter's night in 1998, he had an attack which was later diagnosed as a tiny spot of cancer on his liver. Even though it was only a few cancer cells, it had eaten away the lower edge of Kibbles' liver.

Michael and I were devastated when Kibbles died in my arms in April of that year but, like all animals, we assured him he could come back to our family when he was ready. Typically, animals stay on the other side long enough to heal whatever physical issue they had died from. Just like humans, when they return to Earth too soon, they run the risk of re-imprinting it in the new body.

Within less than a year, we had moved to Colorado, and I began having strong dreams. In every dream it was the same scenario; I saw Kibbles showing me he was coming back but as a long-haired Chihuahua this time, since he was always cold as a short-haired dog. He continued to show me in every dream that he would be the same color combination of black and camel. Another dream showed me that we would have an early snowfall in late September, and I was to begin searching for him the next day. I get my information in specific ways, to say the least.

Weeks went by, then, on the twentieth of July, I awoke to this sweet, beautiful aroma filling my bedroom and clinging to my skin. I ran downstairs to my husband who was making his coffee. "Smell me!" I demanded. He took one sniff and we both charged up the stairs to my bedroom where "new puppy scent" was filling the room. We just stood there smiling because we had a hunch that our beloved Kibbles had just returned to Earth. We called around that morning and told breeders and sellers we spoke with to keep an eye out for any new long-haired Chihuahua puppies that were black and tan in color and to call me should any arrive.

Months later, September rolled around and, sure enough, on September 28, 1999, we awoke to two inches of freshly fallen snow. Immediately, we began contacting breeders and looking for our baby. The problem was, we are animal lovers, and every puppy is a cute puppy, so before this search began, I had given the heavens a few basic instructions. I told the angels that I did not want my new puppy traumatized, so keep him from ever being caged. I also didn't want kids poking at him and scaring him in a pet store, a pet peeve of mine. I am always flabbergasted at the way parents allow children to bully or frighten animals. I wanted to make sure that I got the right puppy, and even though I knew Kibbles' strong personality, I needed something more to ensure we did not take the wrong puppy home. I asked that the puppy be so cute that the very moment I laid eyes on Kibbles, it would physically hurt my eyes. Kibbles was also a very vocal dog who I had taught to say, "Mama," and to sing, so I reminded the heavens of that little nugget, just in case all the other criteria failed.

Autumn was filled with plans we'd made long before the information came about Kibbles. We were eagerly ready to take a trip we'd planned months earlier with our friends. They were driving from Sedona to meet up with us at the annual hot air balloon festival in New Mexico. We searched for weeks to find hotel rooms for us and our dogs, as we each had long-haired Chihuahuas and we were looking forward to letting them play together.

Michael put in a request with his company for vacation time months earlier to secure those few days in October. Michael had worked for Siemens without incident for more than fifteen years but found his new boss, Ron, was a tyrant and took pleasure in sabotaging Michael at every turn. So naturally, after approving Michael's vacation months early, Ron suddenly retracted, telling Michael he could not have the time off. Michael was livid as we scrambled to cancel our hotel room, calling our friends to explain. I was sure something bigger was at work. As I calmed my husband down, I was vehement that there was a spiritual reason we were not intended to leave town.

The very next day, I got a call from a woman who had me on a list to see any new black and tan Chihuahuas. On the other end of the phone, this sweet old lady told me that the puppy she was calling about was supposed to have arrived at their location weeks earlier, but everyone felt he was just too small to take away from the mother.

Michael had left just hours earlier to go to Canon City for a business meeting. Naturally, I called him only to find out that it would be late before he returned home. Calling the puppy owner back within minutes, I discovered that the owner had already gone home for the day and when I told her assistant that I was the woman who she had just called about the new puppy, her response surprised me. "Oh, well, she took that puppy home because she thought he was too small to leave in a cage overnight!"

Bingo! The first of my requests to the universe was complete— not to cage and traumatize my puppy. I suspected then that it was my Kibbles.

The next morning, we raced to her location to meet our little bundle of joy. The owner let us come in and as she closed the large, barn-like doors behind us, I made a request. I ask her to please indulge us; I knew this was going to be a little strange, but I asked her to open the puppy playpen door while we went to the back of the room, where the puppy could not see us. We were anxious to see if our energy would lead this one-pound baby right to us. Within seconds, the most adorable puppy you have ever laid eyes on came toddling down the aisle right into my waiting arms. My eyes instantly hurt beyond belief and my heart was so full, I thought it would explode. Michael stood there, flabbergasted at the instant connection since puppies are typically not very aware when that young. After all the paperwork was finalized, we left with our baby in my arms, snug and secure.

I was in euphoric heaven all evening as we played with this tiny little tyke we fondly named Pokémon. But then something happened I was not expecting nor prepared for. Around 11:00 p.m., this beautiful bundle of joy suddenly became limp and stopped breathing. With the puppy in my arms, my husband hurriedly drove the car to the nearest animal emergency center. A veterinary technician we'd spoken to on the phone met us, grabbing the puppy and rushing him into the back. Our hearts sank as we sat in the empty waiting room, quietly stunned. Had we gotten the wrong dog, and was the universe correcting our mistake? To say the least, our spirits were crushed as we waited in agony for the veterinarian to give us an update.

Within an hour, he came out to tell us something odd, but logical. Dr. Scott informed us that this little puppy had basically gone into a sugar coma because his liver was underdeveloped. When we looked at the X-ray, Michael and I both became weak at the knees. It could have easily been our beloved Kibbles' X-ray. The area of Pokémon's liver which was underdeveloped was identical to where cancer had eaten away at Kibbles' liver a year and a half earlier. Michael and I looked at each other and smiled; we knew it really was Kibbles.

A few minutes later, the door to the lobby opened and our little one-pound bundle of joy ran right over to me. The veterinarian looked shocked and asked, "How long have you had this puppy?"

I replied, "About half a day."

He remarked, "That is unbelievable and pretty rare for a puppy to be so alert and bonded with its owner so quickly."

If only we could have shared our little secret; Pokémon knew us, and we knew him.

The next night I was on the phone with my best friend, sitting in my Lazy Boy rocker, with my feet up and my darling Pokémon sleeping in my lap. The front door opened, signaling Michael's arrival home from work, and the sound startled Pokémon. With my friend on the phone and Michael standing there, Pokémon exclaimed, "Mama Mama!" All three of us screamed almost simultaneously, "It really is Kibbles!"

Pokémon gave me the best thirteen years I have ever known. He sang with me on every song, he was joyful and such an easy baby to love, and he even had his own YouTube videos. I have learned a great deal about animals and how to care for them, but to tell the truth, Pokémon was so human that it was easy to treat him like one. There was not a single day that he did not delight my spirit and fill my heart with everlasting joy. He crossed over the rainbow bridge seven days after his thirteenth birthday in the wee hours of the morning of July 27, 2012. He died in my arms just thirteen days after my beloved fifteen-year-old cat, Tweedy, died a natural death, also in my arms.

Five years later, with yet another nudge from the heavens, I walked into that same family-owned business where two all-white, mop-like sibling puppies sat alone, looking ever so frightened. I was not looking for a pet, much less two, and I was not interested in dogs that would grow to be twice the size of the Chihuahuas I'd spent my life raising. However, I had never seen any like these, so I asked the attendant what they were. She couldn't tell me; she just said they had just arrived and had not even been examined yet.

After a brief chat, I left with my doggy toothpaste but marveled at how these two hovered at each other's side. It was clear they needed one another like they needed breath. I'd never seen twin souls in dogs before, so I was eager to help energetically find them a good home together. I began praying immediately and continued for days. "Please give them a home together; cause the angels to assist in finding the perfect home for these two."

My nights became restless, and dreams came. I could not get those two fluffy snowballs out of my mind. They had long, curly hair—a breed I knew nothing about that looked like they would shed all over the furniture. A week later, I was in the area, so I stopped by the shop, sure they would be gone by now.

I was wrong. There they sat, now in a space with bigger dogs stepping all over them and not looking very well; life in a cage was taking a toll. I had the owner's secretary bring both into the play area and there I sat for more than an hour, playing and bonding with the skittish animals.

It was Christmas time, and even though the son now operated the business, he knew who I was and was more than happy to take a call from me. I asked him if he could assure me that they would be adopted together, if he would be willing to make that a stipulation and criteria for adopting them. Sadly, given the holiday and his goal to find homes for all his dogs, he would not comply. After a long back and forth, we came to an agreement. He would send both puppies over to my veterinarian's office the next morning to have them checked out. I believe I have the best vet in the nation, and I knew he would be thorough and frank with me. I left the store, praying that if I was supposed to have these babies, I was open to it. But if, for whatever reason, they were intended for some other family, I would make peace with that. With spiritual matters, I've learned to never get attached to an outcome.

I arrived at the vet's office the next day and upon entering the room where the puppies were being kept, to my surprise they both leapt into my arms. Unafraid and unleashed, their personalities immediately came to life and revealed the nature inside all that white, fluffy hair. I knew them and they knew me; I'd loved them fully, completely for longer than they'd been white balls of fur. How could I have not seen it the first day I met them? I imagine it is similar to people who have been Mozart or Madame Curie or some other notable walking the Earth with no one noticing them either.

The puppies left the vet's office with me that day, but I was completely unprepared to bring new dogs into my home. Needless to say, for a few challenging weeks, my Chihuahuas were not too pleased. But, eventually, they began to play with the new furry boys.

Today, my home is filled daily with joy and more love than I can handle most days. Yoshi and Yokimon (Yoki) are exact replicas of Tweedy and Pokémon with one caveat; they are white instead of black. Many might dismiss the similarities, but they are so stark, so unique to their former selves, that there is no mistaking who they are. I am blessed and inspired to raise them again, and the connection—like those with their human counterparts—is even more incredible today. It's all about energy as it grows stronger over time.

Yoshi, previously a black tom cat who showed up at our house in Sedona in 1996 and refused to be ignored, today rubs against you like a cat, making a figure 8 in and out of your legs when sitting. He has managed to kill squirrels and mice with flair, just like his old self Tweety, the cat. Yoki, previously Pokémon, sits on my left shoulder just like Pokémon did; he sings, talks, and is very vocal. Their dynamic is something to behold, and those who knew them previously marvel at their behavior, so like their previous incarnations.

Over the years, many clients and those who attend my lectures have asked how they can ensure their "fur babies" return to them or their family. The definitive way to have your pet return to you is simpler than you think. It begins with the connection. Some see a dog, cat, or other household pet as just an object, but most people who love animals view them as souls evolving up the scale in search of love and learning how to be unconditional in theirs.

While that may sound completely absurd to you, all you have to do is look at Instagram sensation Topher Brophy, who is famous for his look-alike dog and daddy pictures. It is common to adopt the type of dog or pet that resonates with you the most, and in many cases, there is a past life connection. Haven't you ever looked at a person who looks like a Poodle or seen someone who looks like a bulldog? There are rich lessons in taking on primitive forms at the beginning of your soul's journey in the Earth plane, and typically, you only do it once.

At this late stage in time, it is no longer necessary since all human souls have completed the primitive and have evolved to the human race.

Your pets want to come back to you most of the time, and will—if you are aware of this option and begin seeding it from the beginning. Dogs and cats, for example, will have similar characteristics but will always return in a body a little larger than the previous one. So, if you had a ten-pound cat, he may return as a twelve or fifteen-pound cat or dog. The body must be large enough to house the expanded soul and comfortable enough for the soul to expand further.

There must always be enough time between the pet dying and returning or, like humans, they will imprint the previous lifetime's injuries or illnesses. In the case of Tweedy and Pokémon, they both died of natural causes brought on by old age. That is a great deal to heal—all the organs shutting down in succession. It took five years and two months for them to sort out their own restoration and find appropriate bodies to incarnate into; siblings were essential for these two since they are so bonded. Prior to their death, Tweedy would compete with my two Chihuahuas, and I even had dreams that he wanted to come back as a dog because the dogs got so much attention.

You can begin soon after a pet has passed and start asking to be shown in your dreams when they are ready to come back to you. If you do that often enough and with pure intention, you will begin to have dreams of your former pet. If you pray with specific guidelines such as type of dog, cat, horse, etc. and couple that with asking to be led and guided back together, you will get your baby back. As I write this, I realize how crazy it sounds, but trust me when I tell you, the animal world is almost identical to humans when it comes to reincarnation. Again, enough Earth time has to be considered before inciting the return of a beloved animal. The consequences of returning too soon for animal or human can be dire. Humans never go backward, but in the beginning, while in infancy stages of consciousness, life began with experimental life forms.

Telepathy plays a key role in connection, whether it is with animals or humans. The more you practice using these principles to create the life you want, the greater your gifts increase. Intuition is developed typically through consistent meditation and practicing mindfulness. The longer you practice meditating, the more connected you become with higher thought and the greater you awaken within. Intuition is innate, but certainty and knowing are elements which must be practiced and achieved for intuitive accuracy. A perfect example of accurate intuition and heightened frequency is what happened with my friend and her dogs recently.

I was working when my girlfriend called in an absolute panic, which is unusual for her. She asked me to use my psychic gifts because her two big dogs were missing, and from what she could deduce, had been gone for at least half an hour. Duke aka Gilbert, the newest of their brood, was barely a year old and stood waist-high, while Jack was eight years old and about the same size. They are both large; Duke is a Pitbull-Great Dane mix and Jack is a Pitbull mix as well. Somehow, they had managed to jump the fence—and to Christy's disbelief, since there were no holes in the fence.

I had never heard her so panicked, so I dropped everything that very minute and ran out of the house. I sped over to her place twenty minutes away and began searching a neighborhood that I was completely unfamiliar with. There are more than five hundred houses in that particular subdivision, and the streets wind around in the most peculiar maze-like ways.

Talking to God and the angels while driving, I repeatedly prayed out loud, or what I fondly call "bombarding the high lines." "The dogs are safe, lead me to them alive and well! Lead me to them alive, show me, show me, show me, lead me to them, lead me right to them, they're safe they're safe they're safe!"

The neighborhood is surrounded by six-lane major thoroughfares on all sides with a consistent flow of heavy, often speeding traffic. As I was driving, I phoned Christy when I found myself lost. I asked if she'd found them and knew from her voice that she hadn't. I told her where I was and asked how to get back to her house. She wanted to know if I was headed north or south, and frankly, I didn't know, so I let the universe lead me. It was a mild day, still warm for early autumn. There were many people walking their dogs, strolling with their babies, and several men were washing their cars, but I didn't stop to ask if anyone had seen them—instead, I relied on my spiritual intuition.

I came to a street ironically named "Balance" and found myself at a T-crossroad, of which I could only turn right or left. Instinctively, with Christy still on the phone, I took a right and continued driving. Suddenly and inexplicably, in the middle of the block, I slammed on my brakes and screeched to a halt. I looked to the right and saw a man washing his car and rolled down my window, asking in a rather loud voice, "Have you seen two big dogs?"

His casual, nonchalant reply was nothing short of miraculous.

"Yes! I have them!"

All Christy heard over the phone was me screaming, "Are you kidding me? Are you kidding me? Christy, I found them, I've got them!"

I left my car in the middle of the street, leapt like a rabbit on fire, and ran into the garage as the owner headed to his backyard to retrieve the two mischievous boys. I lavished hugs and praise on the husband and wife, who had gone out of their way to keep the dogs safe. Within minutes, Christy pulled up behind my car (still parked in the middle of the street), and we proceeded to corral the two happy hounds into her car.

We both knew Duke/Gilbert were behaving just like Christy and Layne's beloved Lucy, a full blood Boxer. Lucy died five years earlier and, as with most animal lovers, the pain was excruciating for the couple. Months earlier, Christy and I started doing the "puppy invocation" and began looking shortly thereafter. Months went by until one day, we decided to meet at PetSmart, where they were having a rescue adoption.

It took seconds; there was Lucy, now a Great Dane-Pitbull mix, rescued off the streets in New Mexico and looking as lost as any rescue I've ever seen. Duke was so broken from his tough life and even with some minor health issues, but once he was back in his old home, he began to thrive. Now approximately two years old, Duke has continued to prove to his family that he is still the mischievous and very vocal hound that Lucy was, constantly talking back to Christy to her chagrin.

What are the odds? In a neighborhood I didn't know, on a street I have never been on in my life, with so many houses blanketing the terrain and so many people walking about— to stop in front of the one house where they were being kept can only be attributed to intuition and energy. Tuning into the Divine Mind where all answers reside, is a gift and an art inside every human being. You must trust your inner guidance in everything you do, including locating dogs that could have just as easily been found dead or stolen. But it was the energy of a familiar nature and listening within that led me to these beautiful creatures. I remain in a constant state of humbled awe; I get just as excited and dumbfounded as those on the receiving end. I'm captivated and aware that if you allow and engage the Divine, practice spiritual principles, and embody love, you can be a useful instrument to those in need.

There is nothing quite as exhilarating as reconnecting with those you've had history with, whether human or animal. Our animals are just like our family members; they too return to us and are guided back by our familiar vibrations and energy. The loss of a pet is one of the most excruciating heartaches a human endures, so it is a comfort to know that, many times, you will see them again.

Chapter 13

Shadow Boxing

As a consummate observer and facilitator of spiritual psychology, I find people purely fascinating. Their interactions and even how they are adorned often speaks louder than their own voice. As a lifelong mystic, empath, and student of body language, I read energy and the body, often revealing everything from depression to malintent. It is the combination of these which over the years has kept me on my toes with clients and guided me when traveling abroad. It is delineation which often defines the total sum of what is occurring at any given moment in time with someone who is struggling in life. There is far more at work within you than what the outer is conveying, and vice versa.

People walk around feeling unworthy or guilty, often never understanding why. I once had a client who told me she stood in the mirror one morning and said, "You're a monster!" She is an unremarkable woman with two small children, a relatively happy home life, and has done nothing extreme in this lifetime to warrant that feeling or to justify those words.

I had another client, who was the epitome of a 60s hippie incarnate—a free spirit in mismatched clothes, no makeup, her tank top laden with stains from her year-old son, and oozing fairy lingo. She was young, intelligent, and all-natural, eating only organic food and taking all the classes she could cram into her schedule.

One day, she came to her session with a list and shared some of the darkest, most sinister thoughts I've ever heard. As I sat listening, my skin was crawling. My blood ran cold; I had to tilt my head slightly back to keep my eyes from popping out. These thoughts were not her imagination running amuck; they were fragments of memories of things she'd done in previous lifetimes which were now beginning to bleed through. I worked with her for more than two years and much was accomplished, resolved, and integrated. However, her frequent use of illegal drugs continues to feed her personal demons today.

You pass people every day, shiny on the outside but dark and full of collective, unconscious memories on the inside. If their thoughts are allowed to fester and grow or go untreated without a qualified counselor or hypnotherapist to help navigate the shadows, they can inadvertently contribute to the underbelly of evil in the world.

You see stories like the Columbine High School or the Sandy Hook Elementary shootings and the spiritually evolved will think, if only Dylan Klebold, Eric Harris, and Adam Lanza had been exposed to a past life regressionist with an expertise in cellular memory. It was reported that both Klebold and Harris were obsessed with Hitler and Nazis. It is quite possible they were Nazis in Germany previously. Adam Lanza walked into Sandy Hook Elementary School on December 14, 2012, in Newtown, Connecticut and murdered twenty-six people, twenty of them children. He had access to firearms and an obsession with mass murders, particularly that of the April 1999 shooting at Columbine. It is possible, if not probable, that he too was a part of the Nazi regime and more than likely knew Klebold and Harris in that previous incarnation. The nature of those who facilitated the mass murder of more than six million Jews, doesn't change dramatically in subsequent incarnations.

We are drawn to the familiar in humans, places, like-mindedness, and other familiar actions. Studies have shown that mass shooters or serial killers often display previous behaviors long before picking up a weapon or plotting a homicide. What forensic psychology fails to consider is what spiritualists have known for eons. Energy is at work; memories which have long since been sleeping or denied can contribute to today's behavior or acts of violence.

Conversely, acts of kindness, extreme examples of heroism, brilliant minds, and exceptionally talented people are, with rare exception, an extension of expertise accumulated from other lifetimes. Reincarnation lends understanding to the children of today, who by the age of two can recite all the presidents' names or are musical prodigies or scholars by age ten. Reincarnation gives understanding to mental illness, addiction, and family feuds or dysfunction. Like karma, the law of cause and effect, aspects from other incarnations often surface when you least expect it.

Understanding reincarnation can also be very liberating to those who are still grieving the loss of a child, parent, or family member years after they've passed. Every day, I see Facebook posts lamenting over the birthday of a mother who died forty years earlier or eulogizing the passing of a father who died twenty-five years earlier.

While I understand the need to share and that many people grieve for decades, I would like to emphasize that their deceased relatives have long moved on, no longer attached to their former identity. That does not, however, negate the need to grieve for as long as you feel the need. There is an old adage which says that grieving is for the living, not for the dead, and it's so true. Of course we miss the people we loved, the personalities of those who moved us or inspired or even cared for us. But it is important to remember they return, often in ways that find their way back to you, the living. No one is ever lost to us; they simply change forms and often return within ten to twenty years after leaving the Earth, many times in your own family or inner circle.

When someone dies, it is rare for the soul to stick around Earth for more than a short time. Mourning limits disincarnate souls and keeps them hovering over you in an attempt to comfort you. Typically, most souls feel elated when free of the human body that they soar beyond this dimension rather quickly. Some linger long enough for you to reconcile yourself to the loss, while others move on swiftly, eager to explore their new world—the heavens and space so enticing. A few will hover in the field just above you (also known as the fourth dimension) and will wreak havoc as a ghost, waking or frightening those they disliked or had strife with.

Souls don't cling to any one identity, birthday, race, name, or profession; all of these are strictly a part of the human condition and ego and have nothing to do with the soul itself. The soul possesses the ability to move gracefully from one lifetime to another, from one existence to another, rarely retaining the remembrance of previous lifetimes when returning to Earth. If we consciously retained the memory of being a king, queen, a henchman, or even a Nazi, it would be too easy to repeat the same behaviors, and often too painful since most souls evolve. Although many do subconsciously have insight as to familiarities with characters or places, when they encounter them on a trip or through reading a book or watching a movie, most dismiss it as coincidence.

What is typical of most souls is that the personality is often consistent throughout every incarnation. If you are shy, you will more than likely remain meek in subsequent lifetimes. If you are bombastic or passionate, those traits will revisit you into future lifetimes. Personality characteristics such as insecurity or deep-seated feelings of inadequacy lend a greater understanding when viewed through the lens of reincarnation. We've all met that girl who on the outside is stunningly gorgeous, only to discover she is chronically insecure. The explanation is simple: you choose a body you think will help you overcome insecurities or other emotional issues, only to discover the body has little to do with the soul and its workings. We've sadly seen cases of many a young person who seem to have everything but is bullied to the point of committing suicide when there was a way to prevent it. Exploring past lives can often save lives. It is worth your time to explore the depths of your soul and uncover any lifetimes which have caused extreme or imbalanced emotions.

The personality and consciousness are intricately intertwined and symbiotic. However, there are some souls who never develop their personality, so it mutates from one incarnation to the other. Those who are inconsistent in forming character and a multitude of virtues are often weak-willed or return with issues that lend to dysfunction or criminal behavior. Additionally, there are souls who repeat negative behaviors in consecutive lifetimes, so it becomes first nature to them. These are the Donald Trump, Ted Bundy, Charlie Manson, Jeffrey Dahmer, and Hitlers of the world. They have found their niche in society and wear it like a badge of honor, often taunting and flaunting their hideousness.

Science has determined that the repetition of certain behaviors hardwires certain parts of the brain, but what is lesser known is that it also hardwires the soul. If you fail to balance lifetimes, exploring only those which feed lower behavior, a darker nature emerges. Conversely, if you choose only lifetimes which navigate the waters of goodness, a naïve and more vulnerable, even weakened nature, emerges.

While there are those on the other side who assist you in what you choose prior to returning, ultimately it is incumbent upon you to choose wisely. Like life on Earth, you have the advantage of researching data and records, but there they are in the form of holograms—a living record for every soul, all lifetimes, all events, and all actions, words, and deeds. These are known as the Akashic records of life, which is what you are tapping into when you meditate to uncover your lifetimes.

Here's a hint; if there is no present-day explanation for the way you feel, it is more than probable that it stems from another time. Whether it's a "phantom" physical ailment, extreme fear, a sense of deep sadness, depression with no obvious cause, a foreboding sense of loss, sudden anxiety, or any number of other abnormalities, there is an explanation. Subtle energy lingers and only becomes problematic when it is attempting to awaken you, giving you an opportunity to deal with it.

By addressing these extreme emotions, they begin to integrate and heal, and you don't have to bring them back with you the next time you incarnate. Many people go through life blaming this, that, or the other for their discomfort, when all they had to do is turn within. There is always an explanation for everything under the sun, always. That explanation is seared into the fabric of your being; it's all inside, and you need only awaken to discover its treasure trove.

Epilogue

The Meaning of Life

Yesterday matters; not so much who you were in previous incarnations, but more, what you learned, what you accomplished, and what you left behind. The past factors in key elements to today's existence, but it's also a roadmap to guide you from driving off a cliff. The mistakes you've made in previous lifetimes, depending on how much impact they had on your body, mind, or consciousness, can be avoided if you're truly awake. We go from one existence to another in an effort to experience all walks of life, to learn how to navigate the terrain and to become the highest version of ourselves possible.

However, never lose sight of the fact that today is what matters most. How much you give, how greatly you love, how much you evolve into a productive, effective human being is elemental. How you treat others, no matter who you are or how much you have, is essential to the very foundation of your continuation and to the continuity of life.

Life ebbs and flows in the liquidity of duality, darkness begets light, light begets darkness, and both are essential to the soul's evolution. While you would probably judge yourself severely if you truly knew all the things you've done in other lifetimes, the beauty of life is that you are your only judge. Your karma, past, and present is the only other voice working in concert with your own internal dialogue. There is no human-like God standing over you to judge you.

When you truly understand the Biblical teachings, especially those of Jesus, you begin to see that his death and resurrection was symbolic to the end of all judgment. You finally understand how his words were designed to empower you to be the gods you were created to be; self-ruling, self-aware, self-awake, and thoroughly connected to the Source of your existence. That source is inside of you awaiting your acknowledgment. Some call it God, some call it the "higher self," and some go so far as to refer to it as a degree of enlightenment. It is, however, innate in all sentient beings.

We all have the same composition and the only delineation between us and the Source is life; you cannot create a soul, thus you cannot take a life. That is the only difference in you and the Light of your creation. Whatever label you need to place on that which cannot be defined is up to you. No judge will stand over you and determine if you're a sinner; it simply doesn't work that way. What I have learned on this and the other side is love—pure love—is the energy of creation. It's far more concentrated and purer than any you encounter on Earth, unless you are hanging out with the Dalai Lama.

Years ago, I was invited to be a contributor for *Huffington Post* during the time that Ariana Huffington still owned it. I had just celebrated my sixtieth birthday and thought I would share some of what I'd learned as an observer and participant on this rich planet. I'd like to share it with you here because these are the principles which, if employed, bring instant positive results to any life. As I approach my sixty-fifth birthday, these resonate even more today.

Penned in 2016, here is an excerpt from "Keys to a Silver Lining."

"In my newfound demographic, I am reminded of Nora Ephron and her book, *I Feel Bad About My Neck*.

Like Nora, I wish I knew the secret to preventing sagging skin as it begins to thin and liquefy, running down the length of my rather short thighs and once toned arms. I don't feel bad about my neck, however. My particular annoyance is the fact that no matter what you do or try your waist circumference will grow proportionate to your age! At full term pregnancy I only weighed 119 pounds so imagine my surprise to look like I am carrying twins today?

Now, don't get me wrong, I am not lacking in self-worth or confidence but honestly, I never expected to be the size of Oompa Loompa, nor did I ever think my bum would take on a shape which has not yet been identified in the mathematical world. As a spiritual teacher I never envisioned becoming so Buddha like; in mind yes, in form, no.

That being said there are some wonderful benefits to aging gracefully...now if only I could remember what they are.

Think of the money I'm saving on hair dye and expensive diets. Pumping my face full of Botox and fillers is not an option because looking like a bloat fish is not on my bucket list. I get all the exercise I need by contorting my body into a pretzel every morning just to get out of my waterbed, which has to burn at least 400 calories.

I find myself referring to people as "folks" and "youngsters" and using "sugar" and "hon" in place of names, which I can no longer remember.

What a treat to find that your body suddenly inflates with more gas than is presently in the tank of your car and you pee more frequently than normal and often without a bathroom in sight.

You realize you will probably never have sex again because the thought of getting naked in front of ANYONE causes you to become faint and slightly nauseous. You can see the headline; "Suffocated by wobbly bits."

What a surprise to find that when you bend over to dry your hair, you dry your fallen breasts at the same time. I have gone from a 36 C to a 36 long in just a few short years.

You can eat anything you want because even if you live to be 100 you are not about to spend a second forfeiting ice cream, sugar or butter. The added benefit is that, "death by chocolate" begins to sound rather appealing.

I have discovered that Ben Gay is an aphrodisiac and Epson salts is as addictive as Crack. And nap time is no longer a choice, it now spontaneously occurs at all hours of the day.

You realize that you don't need a gun to protect yourself because you have a loaded mouth and you know how to use it.

You can also dress in a polka dotted Mumu, put a birds nest in your newly tinted, purple hair and dangle chicken bones from your ears because no one notices you anymore and it's a guaranteed way to ensure that all important senior discount.

Aging gracefully is for the tenacious and courageous. Having a sense of humor is the ultimate benefit and thankfully it is one which comes with age.

Wisdom now overflows like an endless well and even you are surprised at the amount you have despite society's efforts to dumb you down. Most of us have learned more in life's university than we ever did in schools or colleges.

What I find most liberating is knowing that I would not do any of it differently. Every heartache, every betrayal, every hardship, every layer has been rich with texture, dripping with color and intricately woven like a Persian rug, being painstakingly stitched.

I recognize that there are keys to activating the rhythm of flow in life and using them opens every door.

Good character and integrity are the keys to inner peace.

Loving yourself is the key to perfect health.

Giving of yourself is the key to humility.

Serving others is an honor and is the key to inner joy.

Kindness is the key to peace.

Laughter is the key to maintaining a youthful spirit and appearance.

Self-respect is the key to success.

Success is the key to helping humanity and creating a legacy.

Failure is the key to resilience.

Moderation is the key to well-being.

Taking care of your body is the key to preservation.

Crying cleanses the soul and renews the spirit and is the key to purification.

Patience is the key to transformation.

Persecution is the key to greatness.

Forgiveness is the key to grace.

Friends will come and go which is the key to flexibility.

Every race, color and creed is the key to learning and knowledge.

Curiosity is the key to adventure.

Animals are the key to evolving tenderness and compassion.

Nature is the key to the mystical.

Touch is the key to connectivity.

Taste is the key to bliss.

Smell is the key to awareness.

Senses are the key to intuition.

Listening is the key to wisdom.

Closing your eyes is the key to vision.

Meditation is the key to enlightenment.

Prayer and the spoken word are the keys to communication with angels and the Divine and manifest your reality.

I've learned that love is the ultimate teacher, the way shower unto all things; love is the answer to every dilemma and the master key which opens every door in the universe.

The age will arrive, when you realize that you have had your day in the sun and it was amazing, beautiful and full of vistas the meek will never behold.

As you walk into the many new and inviting sunsets, wiser and more contented than ever before, the blessing comes in knowing that sunsets are magnificent, they are replete with a glow the earth savors. Sunsets are completion, the end of the beginning, the beginning of the end; where vision extends into the universe, where creation explodes with magic and mystery and the souls' glow becomes more visible to the Divine.

While a sunrise signifies hope, sunsets demonstrate faith, as you transverse the earth and sky, content with what you have learned and accomplished and eager to blaze a trail and leave a lasting imprint.

Sunsets are the consummate gateway to the stars and it is the stars which light the universe."

Love is the Source and balm of life.

It's in the very air you breathe; it's in the trees as the branches arch and bend in an effort to touch the sky.

It is in the grass that sends ripples of green into your senses, the aroma a potent potion that hearkens you back to your youth.

It is in the lavender fields which beg for you to notice their vibrancy and wait for you to lie down and saturate yourself in wonder, sparking imagination.

That source is the chills you get when you hear truth or the tingle that comes on suddenly when you feel the presence of something greater hovering in the room.

It's the ringing in your ears when angels have joined you, encircling in a dance as they sprinkle light upon you.

It's the hair that stands up on your arms when you are in danger.

It's the churning of your gut when you know you've acted outside of love.

It's the colors you see when you're meditating and instantly know the Divine cord is at its peak intertwining.

It's the sound of silence, the bellow of a thundercloud, the whisper of the wind, the roar of ocean waves as they pound the surf and crash into the breakers.

That source lives in the animals, plants, and insects that feed from the nectar of flowers, too beautiful to describe. And of those flowers, the color spectrum of Source speaks to the variety of your species, every color more beautiful than the last; every voice more powerful than the generations which came before. Every act of love is an expression of the greater sum of Divine energy omnipresent, all-engulfing and all-knowing.

The Source is the peace, the joy, the harmony, the balance, the flow, the wisdom, the anchor, the healer, and the light; it is the spectacular beauty of heaven and Earth. It is you and me and a world of unique human beings: the living, breathing expression of a universe you will only know a tenth of, no matter how many lifetimes you choose to return.

Thank you for purchasing *The Soul's Way ~ The Journey of Reincarnation. How Past Lives Affect Your Present Life and Create Your Future Lifetimes.*

I hope you enjoyed reading it and look forward to hearing from you personally. I would deeply appreciate if you would write an honest review of this book, how it impacted you, or what you gained from reading it at Amazon.com or drop me a personal note at ariaaiam@aol.com.

For personal appearances and inquiries: Ariaaiam@aol.com or www.ariaa.com

Wishing you blessings on your journey to healing, joy, and enlightenment.
Whatever you go, whatever you do, don't forget to use your heart and voice to LOVE OUT LOUD! God bless, take care of each other.

With Beams of Love, Light, and Laughter,

ariaa

About the Author

Ariaa is a word that in Sanskrit, Avestan and Old Persian means "noble" and "excellent". India says the name Ariaa means 'Air'. 'Song or orchestra'. In Hebrew the root, Ari means lion. In God speak Ariaa is "the Alpha, the Omega, the song of life."

Following her 27-minute death in the Alps, Ariaa Jaeger has devoted her life to serving and transforming the lives of millions worldwide. As a spiritual life strategist, advisor and cellular memory pioneer, she combines quantum energy, spiritual principles, spiritual science/psychology, quantum physics and meditation to achieve the highest possible outcome in those with whom she works. Her clientele includes Fortune 500 CEOs, Academy Award-winning actors, celebrities, entrepreneurs, clergy, layman, and students of all ages.

Ariaa received her spiritual wisdom and comprehensive education during her death experience in 1993 which was the ultimate master class in theology, philosophy, spiritual psychology, science, world religions, spiritual principles, emotional and physical body healing and all things that go bump in the night.

Shortly afterward she was invited to speak at the Brain and Mind Symposium in Los Angeles and began a series of classes, workshops and seminars. Since, Ariaa has lectured all over the world and leads global meditations for world peace and transformation. Her meditations and prayers are widely known in the spiritual community for their effective transmission of tangible energy and light. Her original quotes, writings and poetry have impacted millions in social media since 2009.

Ariaa is a tireless advocate for animals and if possible has stated she would own as many animals as she could care for from every species even coining the phrase, "Ariaa's Ark". Additionally, she has sat on the board of several animal charities. Ariaa was chosen as a Love Ambassador for the Love Foundation as the founder of the Love Outloud movement and has been a passionate advocate for human, animal, senior, LGBTQ and environmental rights for more than 30 years.

Ariaa was invited to sing at the United Nations Spirit Awards in 2009 and has been honored with innumerable citations and awards in her nearly 30 year career. She has been featured on a host of radio/podcasts and television shows and has been a contributing writer and columnist for Huffington Post, Thrive Global, Soulwoman and One Tribe magazine.

Ariaa's authenticity, credibility, contagious laughter and sense of humor, her personality, warmth, wisdom, light and passionate love for the earth, animals and people, are a compelling presence. Comments from those she teaches laud her energy as electric and tangible and state her teaching is a living transmission of the highest and purest divine wisdom.

Ariaa currently resides in Colorado with her four beloved dogs, a host of raccoons, squirrels, birds and owls and continues to educate, empower, inspire and enlighten those she works with.

Connect with the Author

To book Ariaa for personal appearances, television, podcast guest appearances, spiritual gatherings, lectures, public speaking, voiceovers, or vocal performances, you may contact Ariaa directly. To book a personal consultation or session with Ariaa, her current contact information can be found on her website: https://www.ariaa.com.

Follow Ariaa on social media:

On Twitter: @AriaaJaeger
https://twitter.com/AriaaJaeger

On Facebook: Ariaa Jaeger
https://www.facebook.com/AriaaJaeger

On LinkedIn: Ariaa Jaeger
https://www.linkedin.com/in/ariaajaeger/

On Instagram: @RealAriaaJaeger

https://www.instagram.com/realariaajaeger/

More Books by Ariaa Jaeger

Ariaaisms Spiritual Food for the Soul,

Crescendo Publishing LLC, 2013

The Book of Ariaa
Quotes for a Luminous Life 2013

The Legend of All One
(children's book currently in production)

Walkins Welcome
A Spiritual Odyssey, 1998 (out of print)

Essentials for Ascension, 1993 (out of print)

A higher way of thinking,
a more evolved way of living
and a more loving way of being.

ariaa®

ariaa.com

Bibliography

Above Suspicion, directed by Steven Schachter (HBO, 1995).

Balzac, Honore de. *La Comedie Humaine (The Human Comedy)*. New York: NYRB Classics, 2014.

Chopra, Deepak. *Ageless Body, Timeless Mind: The Quantum Alternative to Growing Old*. New York: Harmony, 1994.

Cockell, Jenny. *Yesterday's Children*. London: Piatkus, 1993.

Das, Subhamoy. "The Spiritual Quest of George Harrison in Hinduism." https://www.learnreligions.com/george-harrison-and-hinduism-1769992, 2019.

Ephron, Nora. *I Feel Back About My Neck And Other Thoughts on Being a Woman*. New York: Knopf Doubleday Publishing, 2008.

Ford, Henry, interview, *San Francisco Examiner*, 1928.

"The Global Consciousness Project Meaningful Correlations in Random Data." https://noosphere.princeton.edu, 1998-2015.

Goethe, Johann Wolfgang Von, translated by Walter Kaufmann. *Goethe's Faust*. New York: Anchor, 1962.

Harrison, George. *Circles*, (song lyrics). Poland: Sm Publishing, 1982.

Hidden Figures, directed by Theodore Melfi (20th Century Fox, 2016).

Jaeger, Ariaa. "Keys to a Silver Lining." https://www.huffpost.com/entry/keys-to-a-silver-lining_b_57607e88e4b-02081542f8111?ncid=engmodushpmgooooooo4, 2016.

Jaeger, Ariaa. *Ariaaisms: Spiritual Food for the Soul.* Ariaa. com, 2013

Jung, Carl. *The Red Book.* New York: W. W. Norton & Co, 2009.

Lewis, Michael. *The Big Short: Inside the Doomsday.* New York: W. W. Norton & Co, 2010.

Masefield, John. *Selected Poems.* Manchester: Carcanet Press, 1984.

Matthiessen, Peter. *The Snow Falcon.* New York: Viking Press, 1978.

"Melissa McCarthy & Ben Falcone Get a Dreamy Surprise from Mark Wahlberg." https://www.youtube.com/watch?v=-pHuT_inC1zE&list=UL1ykmpYhj1j4&index=693, Ellen Degeneres Show, 2020.

Morely, John. *The Works of Voltaire.* New York: Andesite Press, 2017.

Nikhilananda, Swami. *Vivekananda: A Biography.* New York: Ramakrishna Vivekananda Center, 1989.

Powell, Alvin. "When Science Meets Mindfulness." *The Harvard Gazette* (https://news.harvard.edu/gazette/story/2018/04/harvard-researchers-study-how-mindfulness-may-change-the-brain-in-depressed-patients/, 2018.

Rosenbloom, Joseph. "Martin Luther King's Last 31 Hours: The Story of His Final Prophetic Speech."

The Guardian (https://www.theguardian.com/us-news/2018/apr/04/martin-luther-king-last-31-hours-the-story-of-his-prophetic-last-speech), 2018.

Rumi, Jalalu. "I Died as a Mineral." In The Mystics of Islam, Edited by Reynold A. Nicholson, p. 125. Woodland: Murine Press, Reprint 2007.

Ryan, Charles. *H. P. Blavatsky and the Theosophical Movement*. Pasadena: Theosophical University Press, 1975.

Singer, Isaac Bashevis. *Stories From Behind the Stove*. Tel Aviv: I.L. Peretz, 1970.

Stevenson, Ian, M.D. *Children Who Remember Previous Lives*. Jefferson: McFarland, 2000.

Stevenson, Ian, M.D. *Where Reincarnation and Biology Intersect*. Westport: Praeger, 1997.

"Study on the Maharishi Effect: Can Group Meditation Lower Crime Rate and Violence?" https://tmhome.com/benefits/study-maharishi-effect-group-meditation-crime-rate/, 2016.

"Summary of 13 Maharishi Effect Published Studies." https:// research.miu.edu/maharishi-effect/summary-of-13-published-studies, 2020.

Titanic, directed by James Cameron (Paramount Pictures & 20th Century Fox, 1997).

Torrey, B (Ed). *The Writings of Henry David Thoreau: Journal 1837-1846, 1850-Nov 3 1861*. Boston: Houghton Mifflin, 1906.

bbc.com, "TransAsia Crash: Survivors' Stories." https://www. bbc.com/news/world-asia-31144422, 2015.

Tucker, Jim, M.D. *Return to Life: Extraordinary Cases of Children Who Remember Past Lives*. New York: St. Martins Press, 2013.

"Washington Crime Study Research Findings." www.worldpeacegroup.org/washington_crime_study.html, June, 1993.

Weiss, Brian, M.D. *Many Lives, Many Masters: The True Story of a Prominent Psychiatrist, His Young Patient, and the Past-Life Therapy That Changed Both Their Lives*. Fireside, 1988.

Whitman, Walt. *Leaves of Grass*. New York: Viking Press, 1959.

The Zohar, an English Translation. London: Socino Press, 1934.

Acknowledgments

Special thanks to Sarah Rabel for her stellar bibliography.

Special thanks to Christy Eck Myers and Christy Leigh Photography for the About the Author photo and front cover image of Ariaa.

Thank you also to my ex-husband, Michael, for his loving and generous support throughout our 30-year journey together.

Thank you to Ruth Paulson, whom the Holy Spirit once termed my "hand maiden," for being an amazing friend of 28 years, my constant confidant, a wise sage, and a powerful energy worker.

Made in the USA
Columbia, SC
24 July 2021